Lisa Roukin, a Le Cordon Bleu chef, and known also through 'Cook with Lisa', has been demonstrating healthy, contemporary cooking to London's young professionals, families and children since 2008. That same year she was a finalist on "The F Word" leading her to realise that she wanted to be her own boss in the kitchen!

Her career in the catering trade has included: Mirabelle, L'Escargot, Quo Vadis, The Ivy and Le Caprice. She currently provides the world's largest online supermarket, Ocado, with gluten free recipes.

Going forward, Lisa aims to continue on the healthy path she has found. Her emphasis also continues to be on creating nourishing recipes that encourage people of all ages and skill levels to cook together.

MY RELATIONSHIP *with* FOOD

ISBN – 978-1-910256-86-2

Author	Lisa Roukin
Creative & Design	Spiffing Covers
Photographer	David Munns
Prop Stylist	Victoria Allen
Food Stylist	Emily Kydd
Stylist	Jude Lobb
Make-up	Rina Steinberg
Hair	Carlos Alves
Food	Ocado
	Panzers Fruit
	Bifulco Butchers
	JA Corney Fish
	Menachems Butchers

Notes for the reader.

I have endeavoured to provide healthy, gluten-free recipes. Gluten does appear in many guises and it will be up to you to check labels. There are dishes containing dairy products but I've designed them so you can omit these ingredients or substitute with others. As always, if you are concerned, check with the manufacturer.

My aim is to reduce the amount of refined white sugars and there are only a handful of recipes that include icing sugar. Please also note that some recipes contain nuts, which should be avoided if you have an allergy.

Garnishes and serving suggestions are all optional and based on what works best for you. I have omitted using white rice as brown is my preferred choice.

I do use coconut oil in my recipes. I tend to use pure coconut oil that doesn't have an intense smell of coconut. You can substitute for sunflower or groundnut oil if no allergies or your preferred choice of oils.

The times given in the preparation and cooking method are an approximate guide. Cooking times may also vary; you may need to adjust the temperature according to your oven manufacturer's guide.

Printed and bound in UK By Spiffing Covers

Website reference
www.myrelationshipwithfood.com
www.cookwithlisa.com
www.spiffingcovers.com
www.foodphotography.co.uk
www.emilykydd.com
www.ocado.com
www.whatwearwhen.biz
www.makeupbyrina.com

ocado.com
The online supermarket

Thank you to ocado.com for kindly providing the fabulous ingredients to create all the recipes featured in this cookbook. You can find a selection of my recipes at ocado.com/recipes (author 'Cook with Lisa'), and you can order all the ingredients at the touch of a button.

MY RELATIONSHIP *with* FOOD
100 recipes to nourish mind, body & soul

Lisa Roukin

Dedication

My Relationship with Food is dedicated to my Mother and Father. With their patience and guidance, this dream of mine has become a reality.

To my Mother

Not only are you my best friend, I am extremely grateful for the incredible relationship we share. From a young child, I have watched you create wonderful, memorable family meals, which have brought smiles to all who ate them. I've always aspired to cook like you and bring happiness to all my nearest and dearest. I have fond memories of shopping for food and cooking with you and grandma. I am so grateful that three generations of us can still cook together. You've been a wonderful mentor to me both inside and out of the kitchen. I cannot thank you enough for your support, guidance, encouragement and love.

To my Dad

I am so proud that we have shared the journey of creating this book together. You have dedicated so much time ensuring that it highlights all the wonderful dishes you love. I have enjoyed you being with me every step of the way.

You gave me a wonderful childhood packed with sharing your LOVE of food at all meal times. Thank you for being my chief taster and the pillar of my support.

And most of all I am truly grateful to you both for letting me experiment in the kitchen.

Love, Lisa x

Contents

Introduction

This isn't an ordinary cookbook. Yes, there are delicious recipes, gorgeous photos and clear instructions. But that's where the similarity ends. This book is personal. It's my story of how I've been able to manage my relationship with food.

I can hear you saying 'relationship with food' what does that mean? But, think about it: Consider how often you've been sitting at a table and someone announces 'I don't eat meat', 'I've just lost three stone get that fudge cake away – quick!', 'I don't eat green vegetables' or admits that they weren't fed well as a child. These are all types of food relationships.

Now, think about a bad day at work and that desire to come home to a frozen triple-stuffed pizza and half-bottle of wine. Or remember being 'treated' with an ice-cream cone or a sticky pudding after an insipid school dinner? Food in these cases has altered from *sustenance* to *comfort*, and the relationship with food has shifted.

If a personal relationship goes wrong in your life, there are a number of steps – often painful ones – you can take to help you move on and regain your independence and self-esteem.

But if – like many of us – your relationship with food is not healthy, you have to face that 'relationship' at least three times a day for the rest of your life.

Worse yet, you have to decide what to put on your plate and in your mouth. You may have trouble when going out to eat with family or friends. But you don't have to continue like this.

Here's where I'd like to come in and change things.

I've gone through some tough food relationships, and as you read on, I'll share with you tips on becoming healthy and nourished. My journey isn't that unusual, but it does have a happy ending.

After all, it is not all about 'what' you are eating but how you can make small alterations to help your relationship with food become an enjoyable one.

Our journey starts here.

Lisa Roukin

My Relationship with Food

Eat what nourishes your body, do what nourishes your soul, think what nourishes your mind.

If you have a healthy relationship with food, the above advice is wonderful. But what if you don't? There comes a time, especially in teenage years, when we realise that we can't control everything around us.

However, for some of us comes the understanding that we *can* absolutely control what we put into our mouths. We can change the way our bodies look by eating less. We can control what the scales say. We can control how our jeans fit. And let's be honest. It is a powerful feeling.

But… It can be lonely and restrictive.

It makes us angry because we are not enjoying what everyone else is eating. It takes so much energy and 'mind-time' to plan what we are going to eat and how we are going to avoid the spectre of unwanted calorie-laden food. Imagine this unhealthy relationship with food continuing into adult years. Now, there are calls to dinner party hosts asking what they are planning on serving at their party, there are demands for 'special' foods, there are avoidance tactics when birthday cakes appear or when

alcohol is served. For me, for too long, this was my relationship with food.

Early years

In a light-hearted manner, my mother has said 'perhaps giving Lisa flour and butter to play with as a child wasn't a great idea'. She wasn't commenting on my baking skills, but the fact that, early on, I learned to love foods which would later negatively affect my life.

My early relationship with food was based on comfort and the need for internal nourishment. While I was raised in a very close family, I still had a void that needed filling. I was shy and with that I also lacked confidence. I found joy in helping (and snacking) in the kitchen where the atmosphere was warm and safe. Eating gave me comfort. So I did a lot of it. You can guess what came next. I became a fat child. In fact, when I was 13, I weighed as much as my father, 180 pounds!

Not unexpectedly, I was teased about my weight by my classmates. This made me unhappy and I ate even more. It wasn't a healthy cycle. In my teen years, I realised that I was hiding behind this weight and I set about doing something about it. My relationship with food changed. Food was no longer a comfort but became the enemy.

I turned my back on all the foods that had made me 'happy'. Worse yet, I couldn't see the difference between 'good' foods and those that had fostered the weight gain. To me, food was my adversary and the only way I could 'win' was to be in control. For a short while, I was the victor. I changed from the overweight kid to the thin teenager. I got attention and I gained confidence.

I felt like the proverbial ugly duckling that had turned into a swan.

But what I didn't realise was that this new relationship with food was actually controlling *me*. Being thin didn't seem enough – I needed to be thinner. I was so fearful of that 'fat child' reappearing that I stuck to my food avoidance and suffered.

Little did I realise that my new relationship with food was arguably more destructive than the overeating.

I wasn't clear about eating sensibly and I was excluding most food groups from my daily diet. At this stage in my life, I had a really negative outlook on food and, in turn, my actions deprived me of what I loved most in life – cooking, entertaining and relaxed eating with family and friends. I wasn't able to 'go with the flow' at family gatherings or going to restaurants, I always wanted to know what the menu was, what I could eat, and how the food would be cooked. This need for control even extended to what time we would be eating! Often, I would get so frustrated with all the anxiety I was causing

myself and everyone else with my behaviour that I would end up not going out at all.

I was the one who lost out and it got to a stage where this unhealthy pattern was not benefitting my happiness at all. This bad food relationship meant that I was excluding myself from enjoying life with my family and friends.

Finally, I decided that enough was enough and something had to change.

I needed to understand why I was taking these negative actions. And like any relationship that is faltering, it was useful to think about 'why' my behaviour had evolved. I spoke to the people closest to me

and was surprised at the level of worry I had caused. I considered my insecurities about being overweight, about not having the new friends I had made post-weight loss, and the fear I had about becoming that 'ugly duckling' again if my new skinny status wasn't maintained. This wasn't an easy time and changes didn't happen overnight!

My career in food

My life took an unusual turn at this point. I understood I had issues around food and eating and yet cooking was at the core of my happiness! Ironically, my career had taken me into the catering industry and I had worked in some of London's finest restaurants including Mirabelle, L'Escargot and Quo Vadis. I even headed the events department at Le Caprice.

Yet, in private, I was struggling on a daily basis with this relationship with food – and I was always surrounded by it. The glamour of these jobs also meant that my appearance was even more important than before. I continued to struggle obsessively to find the balance between 'thin' and 'happy'.

But then a little old lady changed my life. My grandmother. After a particularly stressful day, she asked me to sit down and tell her what was wrong. I told her about the confused feelings I had about eating, about work and my future. She looked at me and simply asked, 'What makes you happy?' I looked back at her and replied, 'Cooking'. She smiled and simply said, 'Then cooking is what you should do!' With the support of my family, I enrolled at the prestigious Le Cordon Bleu cooking school and started on a road that would change my life.

For the first time, I realised that food preparation was only half of the issue – I also needed to learn *how to eat*. In a professional kitchen, portion control is at the heart of preparation. You consider how food is presented. You learn about nutrients and about balancing not only flavours, but food groups. Slowly a new relationship with food was beginning to form, and it was an exciting and creative time.

I gradually realised that with my new food knowledge, I didn't have to choose between my ideal weight and being 'happy'. I could have both!

Through reading, experimenting and tasting, I had identified what worked best for me and my body; creating recipes that gave me the satisfaction and 'comfort' that I wanted, but were balanced and nutritious at the same time. Over the last few years, I am proud to say, my relationship with food has become what it should be.

Like I said before, these changes didn't happen overnight. It has taken time, but I'm there! You can be too.

A healthy relationship or let's say 'informal action plan'

Before we start, there's something I'd like you to understand: I am not a person who chomps on carrots asserting their superiority over cupcakes! This is not about a path to being thin, it's about becoming healthy and nourished.

Although, initially, it may sound like it is about 'excluding' foods, the core of the advice is about getting a balance and changing the way you approach eating.

Whether you've been diagnosed with coeliac disease, are gluten/wheat intolerant or want to transform your diet, my approach is simple. I want to share what has worked for me. In other words, you don't have to make all the decisions yourself. You don't have to read all the conflicting advice in health magazines. You don't have to make a vow

never to eat chocolate cake again. I'm just suggesting that you tip your eating patterns toward 'healthy'.

What's healthy? Here's what I've found

Decrease

- refined sugar
- white starchy carbohydrates
- animal fat and cream
- 'rewarding' yourself with calorie-laden food
- giving yourself a hard time if you fall 'off the wagon'!

Increase

- cooking with colourful vegetables
- the amount you cook at any given time
- the variety and types of food you eat
- texture into your cooking by adding nuts and seeds
- time spent on yourself. Take a walk each day, sit in the sunshine, or just read a book in a quiet place

Taking care of yourself

You'll find in the 100 recipes contained here that I've focussed on dishes that do not contain gluten, and an overload of carbohydrates or refined sugar. This style of eating has worked for me and I've found, with experimentation and sneaky 'market-research' on family and friends that you can still enjoy tasty, wholesome food without these ingredients.

There are technical and scientific reasons for these choices, but the main reason I've made this decision is that eating this way has made me feel better. Lighter. More clear-headed. My energy levels have become steadier and I don't find myself with my head on the desk by 3pm! And, I haven't gained back the weight. A definite bonus.

I hope those of you who love gluten and all things starchy can find something to enjoy here too. I hope it encourages you to cut down on processed wheat and sugar. Do it. See how you feel. You won't feel worse… Trust me. You will only feel better.

Fortunately, there has been a rise in demand for healthier options and supermarkets, restaurants and even neighbourhood coffee shops are stocking larger selections of healthy products. This style of eating is not 'alternative' anymore but absolutely becoming mainstream.

'Take care of your body. It's the only place you have to live'

Your journey toward a healthy relationship with food: top ten tips

1. I CAN RESIST ANYTHING EXCEPT TEMPTATION

Perhaps Oscar Wilde had a point, why keep unhealthy food in your house? Check all the labels of the food in your house. If 'sugar' is listed in the top five ingredients, throw it out! Instead, ensure you have your favourite ingredients available in your fridge and store cupboards. Check 'best by' dates, too.

2. PLAN AHEAD

The key to happiness in a gluten-free diet is planning. Without forward thinking, you will find yourself eating convenience foods in the shape of burgers, pizza, sandwiches or pre-prepared foodstuffs that will not only contain gluten but will undoubtedly be high in fat.

3. NOURISH YOUR MIND

De-clutter your thoughts with a silent break, walk or meditation.

4. GOOD FOOD IS GLUTEN-FREE

Vegetables and fruit do not contain gluten. Meat, poultry and fish don't contain gluten. We have an abundance of ingredients to cook with, and even better, they're the kinds of foods we should be eating.

5. MAKE IT BIG

As convenience foods usually contain gluten, to avoid falling into the 'I'm hungry now and I don't have the patience to cook at 6pm' trap, I make a big batch of soup, about 10 portions. When it's ready I break it down into takeaway containers and freeze it. Puréed soups work best like pumpkin, parsnip or sweet potato. They are delicious and filling and can work well for lunches or dinners. Making your own food is definitely the way to go; aside from being cheaper, you have total control of what is going into your body.

6. BE AWARE

Conscious eating means eating foods that agree with your body. It is an inner wisdom of the body. It is your body communicating what is nourishing you and what is not. It is that simple.

7. ...IS ALL YOU NEED

Season everything with love, what you put in is what you get out.

8. THE ONLY WAY IS UP

One small positive thought in the morning can change your whole day. Eat clean, stay clean! Every new day is another chance to change your life.

9. ENJOY!

Start as you mean to go on, remember that eating should be an enjoyable process. Make it a regular habit to prepare your meals with time and relaxation. Be totally present with the preparation of your meals, and don't do anything else at the same time. When you eat, only eat. Feel how the food tastes, smells, relish the colours, feel the different textures in your mouth.

10. FEEL

Perhaps the most intimate relationship each of us will ever have is not with another person – instead it's between our bodies and our food.

Meet Lisa Roukin, Your questions, my personal experience.

Q. What inspired you to write this book?

After you've been on a hard journey, you want to share what you've learned. I see a lot of people struggling with their relationship with food, and it's only natural to want to help. It was in this spirit that I found myself offering stories about my relationship with food to my cooking classes.

I'd also realised that this focus on healthy eating and exercise had worked for me for a number of years. I hadn't regained the weight I had lost. I still had the vitality I had when I began eating this way, and I had more than 100 recipes in my personal collection. A cookbook was a natural extension of all these things.

As a chef, I've gained experience in food preparation and menu planning. As a person, I've struggled with a bad relationship with food in the past. The cookbook details my journey toward healthy eating and my philosophy of nourishment which I've found strikes the best balance between food enjoyment and health.

We can all find happiness regardless of our weight or body shape – the key is finding a way of eating that benefits body, mind and soul. *Choose* to eat well.

Q. Earlier in this book, you talk about a 'bad relationship' with food. Bad relationships aren't that easy to break. How did you do it?

After I had lost the 4 stone as a teenager, I obsessed about my weight constantly worrying about calories and becoming heavy again. In order to ensure that I had complete control over what I ate, I abstained from parties, social situations and even family meals.

Looking back, I lost out on a lot of good times. I finally sought help for my food issues and was advised to keep a notebook to write down my thoughts before and after meals. Slowly, I began to realize that I was using food as a reward. Experts agree that emotional eating is a habit, it is a behaviour we have learned, probably in childhood, and it comes from the happy feelings connected to eating special or 'naughty' food.

But food is not naughty, it is not cheeky, it is not rebellious. Those things are emotions inside us. The food is just food. And if this eating behaviour is learned, then it can be unlearned too. Problems with eating are rarely about the food itself. Emotional eating is not usually about greed, it is about fulfilling a different need.

Q. What do you think are some of the reasons for these unhealthy relationships with food?

The most common reasons for overeating are: to reward or indulge yourself; when you need love or attention; and to relieve boredom.

Emotional eating is not so much about what you eat; it is about when and why you eat. Ever scoffed a chocolate bar without even tasting it? Ever had a full meal, but then an hour later, you're nibbling and snacking on something else? You probably weren't hungry, but you were lonely, stressed, unhappy, or frustrated.

Comfort eating is not a new concept. Freud considered overeating to be the manifestation of a trauma or significant event in the oral stage of childhood development. Any woman who suffers PMT can relate to the concept of emotional (or hormonal) eating. And this is why diet plans often fail. I'm not knocking weight loss regimes or diet clubs. I think they all have a positive role to play, and really do work for some people. I just don't think they are enough because if you eat to negate your emotions, then counting calories will not work, and the next time you go to a 'weigh in' you may add 'feeling guilty' or a 'bit of a failure' to those negative emotions because you didn't stick to the plan.

But overeating doesn't mean that you didn't know what to do, just that the eating was driven by an unconscious force, an inner voice you could not switch off. So, you go home, defiant, and eat something bad. Not because you are hungry, but have an urge to fulfil that emotional need that hasn't been satisfied. And this is a very negative cycle. For me, I learned early on that food was a reward.

I also know that an emotional low – like a relationship break-up, or being stressed at work – can unconsciously lead to seeking something 'nice'. Something that tells me I am special, am 'ok'. And this is the merry-go-round I've fought to get off! Understanding the events leading to this bad relationship is key to taking back control of your eating habits. Writing it down helps you to see your patterns more clearly.

Q. Any advice for people who continue to struggle with these relationships with food?

Be patient and don't beat yourself up when you fall off the wagon. Make changes gradually and you are more likely to stick

to them longer-term. For instance, you wouldn't wake up and run a marathon without months of training so why should you jump into a 'radical' diet and expect it to work immediately? Slowly start alternating better foods. 'Better' in this case means healthy - foods that won't give you energy spikes. Be good to yourself.

To start with, we all know that the best way to lose or maintain weight in a healthy, sustainable way is through a combination of diet and exercise. But for large numbers of us, that isn't as easy as it sounds. We know what we should be doing but we just can't find the willpower to make the change. And we don't need the large helping of guilt and failure that comes with not following a

diet! How many of us start the New Year with good intentions, but just a few weeks in, all it takes is a bad day at work, or cold, miserable weather and before you know it we are 'treating' ourselves to that takeaway for dinner because 'I'm too tired to cook'. I'll bet that sounds familiar.

And that's because of both our relationship with food and lack of planning.

The best way to succeed is to be organised. Ensure that the food that is good for you is actually in the house! Try slowly decreasing the amount of refined sugar and flour you have in your diet. Experiment with the time of day you eat and the quantity you eat. Listen to your body.

Q. Almost all the recipes in the cookbook are gluten-free. What is the thinking behind this?

While I am not a dietician, I've experienced the many health benefits of eating a cleaner and gluten-free diet. I'm now embracing the elimination of wheat/gluten. I want to educate people to understand that you can still make wonderful, tasty and wholesome looking dishes using wheat-free substitutes for favourite foods and sleep well knowing that they are full of goodness! And not every dish you make has to get its carbohydrates from starches since fruits and vegetables contain forms of them.

People who love gluten could really notice the difference that a reduced gluten diet makes. It may even encourage those with weight/digestion problems, poor skin, little energy or low immune systems to cut out/cut down on gluten. Once you've tried it, you won't want to go back to feeling sluggish and tired. The health benefits can make such a difference to your everyday life.

Q. Here's the tough question, if you are not eating bread, what do you have for breakfast?

No excuses! Try Coconut Porridge, Israeli Salad with scrambled eggs, or Bircher Muesli. You could also be a bit radical and have a vegetable omelette, or a frittata with quinoa. In some Mediterranean countries they eat eggs, olives and tomatoes for breakfast and in the Far East, they even have chicken soup! Small changes can improve your energy levels a lot. Breakfast is the perfect time to set a good standard for the day ahead.

Q. Now for an even harder question, how do you ensure you eat healthy food when you are going out for dinner or to someone's house? What if you are handed a piece of cake at someone's birthday party?

If you go out, stick to protein and vegetables. For example, have grilled chicken with salad at lunch or ask for cooked vegetables at dinner. You can even do this with a hamburger – just skip the bun and ask for salad instead of chips. Most restaurants will deal with this request without extra charges or hassles (it doesn't cost them any extra which is half the battle!).

You can even go out for a Sunday lunch – just skip the potatoes & Yorkshire pudding

and you can eat everything else. (You may want to ask if the gravy is gluten-free if you have allergies).

Just be sure you haven't waited too long to eat. If you have, it will be much harder to refuse the basket of bread. Once again, plan ahead.

Look for menu items that feature texture – such as salads with nuts. At home, fill your plate with colourful vegetables. Soon you will see eating sweet potatoes and red peppers as 'treats' because if you reduce your sugar intake – you'll notice how naturally sweet nature can be! And as far as that birthday cake is concerned, the trick is to be gracious. Say 'It looks delicious,' but check that it's gluten-free, and make sure that a small slice is cut! As they say; 'a moment on the lips, a lifetime on the hips'.

Or, if it is a good friend, try the truth. 'I find it difficult keeping a healthy balance in my life, please don't tempt me.'

Q. When you entertain at home, do you stick to a gluten-free menu?

Yes. When the food is fresh, healthy, nutritious and delicious people don't notice! In fact, the usual reaction is 'I've never had this before, may I have the recipe?'

The non-cheater's 'cheat sheet'

Another secret to having a good relationship with food is knowing how to substitute 'healthy' foods to satisfy cravings. The hard part is knowing what to substitute.

To make it easier for you to use this book, here are some healthy alternatives to some of the most commonly requested dishes. Soon I hope, you'll be craving the new dishes instead! Remember - plan ahead and have as many of the recipes that store well on-hand in case hunger strikes without warning! I always have homemade bircher muesli in the fridge for when I just *need* something sweet and quick!

I really want	I'll try this instead
French Toast with Maple Syrup	Bircher Muesli, Homemade Granola or Individual Granola & Berry Pots
English Fry Up	Shakshuka or Baked Eggs in Portabello Mushrooms
Macaroni Cheese	Courgette Spiralised Spaghetti with Aubergine Sauce
Deep Fried Chicken	Baked Cornflake Chicken Breast with Pan Fried Jersey Royals, Shallots & Rosemary
Pizza with Pepperoni	Cauliflower Pizza Base with Blue Cheese Walnut & Pear
Four Cheese and Mushroom Tart	Courgette & Shiitake Mushroom Quinoa Frittata
Deep Fried Courgette/Zucchini	Oven Baked Asparagus in Parmesan & Almond Crust
Bag of Crisps	Baked Curly Kale or Brussels Sprout Chips
Bar of Milk Chocolate	Raw Chocolate Brownie
Sticky Toffee Pudding with Custard	Lemon and Almond cake
Ice Cream Sundae	Banana Ice Cream with Halva
Cheesecake	Raw Blueberry Cheesecake

SPRING

seasonal moods

Revive! Like a door opening onto a brightly lit stage, Spring arrives. There's real drama as the first brightly coloured flowers surface and the lightest of green leaves appear on trees. The sky becomes clearer and brilliant blue again.

And with the additional sunshine comes a new harvest: the annual wonder of fresh asparagus as their tiny verdant heads reach through the soil to the warmth above; cauliflower, like a vegetable bouquet, is also in season with its versatile personality. It's 'A-list' friend, kale, packed with flavour and goodness adorns grocers' shelves.

Menus become lighter with the lifting of mood and it is also a time devoted to regaining energy. Spring is a time to 'clear out', de-clutter and get rid of anything that you no longer need or want. Embrace and allow the energy of new beginnings to flow in.

BANANAS They are the most popular fruit in the UK and a powerhouse of nutrition – high in potassium, B6 and magnesium. Try freezing them for the ultimate smoothie ingredient.

MINT There are 25 different species of mint but all have the cool, fresh scent which is instantly recognisable. As a food, the benefits of mint are often linked to the stomach, not least because it can relieve the symptoms of indigestion and muscle spasms.

CASHEWS Not only delicious as a snack or garnish, cashews also have a lower fat content than most other nuts, with over half their fatty acid content appearing as heart-healthy monounsaturated fats, similar to those found in olive oil. Makes wonderful nut butter, too!

ALMONDS Originating in the Middle East in both sweet and bitter varieties, almonds are particularly good for you. They are high in calcium - great news for anyone who doesn't eat dairy products.

QUINOA Pronounced 'keen-wah', technically quinoa is not a true grain but a seed related to spinach and Swiss chard. In food preparation think of using it in the same way you would rice. It is a powerhouse of nutrition containing protein, calcium, iron, vitamin E and B vitamins.

KALE If there could ever be such a thing as an 'A-list' vegetable then it has to be kale. It's loved by nutritionists for its high calcium, vitamin K, vitamin C and omega-3 fatty acid content. No wonder it has been touted as the best green veggie around.

CAULIFLOWER Mark Twain called it 'broccoli with a college education' but cauliflower also offers 80% of your daily requirement of vitamin A. Try it in curries, salads and shaved finely with a touch of flavoured oil.

ASPARAGUS British asparagus is worth waiting for as its flavour is hard to beat. When shopping, look for tightly furled tips and shoots that are straight and firm.

Banana & Chia Seed Pancakes

Perhaps my ultimate challenge - creating
pancakes without flour & sugar!

....

{makes 6 pancakes}

ingredients

2 large bananas, (mash ¾ of the
bananas, keep the ¼ for garnish)

2 large eggs, beaten

1 tsp chia seeds

2-4 tsp coconut oil

2 pinches salt

½ tsp baking powder

garnish

banana

blueberries

agave nectar

2 handfuls pecans

Preparation time - 20 mins, cooking time - 5 mins

Mash ¾ of the bananas until smooth, then add the egg and beat well.

Stir in the chia seeds, baking powder and salt and leave to rest for 5 minutes.

Heat a non-stick frying pan on a high heat and place a touch of coconut oil to both the pan and a spatula (coating the spatula will help when turning over the pancakes).

Turn the heat down to medium, pour a circle of the batter into the pan. I use about 60ml of the mixture per pancake.

Cook until golden brown on the underside (approx. 1 minute), then flip over and cook until golden brown on the other side (about 30 seconds).

Once you've cooked all 6 pancakes, stack them back on each other to warm through in the hot pan, but take the pan off the heat.

Serve warm with remaining ¼ of the banana sliced, blueberries, crushed pecans and agave nectar.

Yum...

LISA'S TIP

My favourite food of all time? Pancakes. Hands down. But traditional pancakes aren't exactly nutritious. So I wanted to figure out an alternative! Eggs and a banana…. that's all! Two of my favourite foods come together to create a simple, yet, scrumptious pancake. It's hard to believe that you don't need flour, milk or refined sugar to create a lovely, light and kid-approved pancake. Although delightful, don't be expecting your run-of-the-mill carb-filled pancake. These have more of an eggy crepe-like texture, which is equally appealing. If you're used to eating clean healthy foods, you will more than likely LOVE these. Low-calorie, high-protein, gluten-free and wheat-free…. what's not to love? Not only do they make a quick and easy breakfast, but they're also the perfect pre or post-workout fuel. Try adding some other types of berries and nuts. Be adventurous with your fillings or just keep it plain and simple! You could also add a touch of baking powder if you like them slightly thicker.

Almond Milk

Nut milk is heavenly – sweet, mild
and gentle on the stomach.

{makes a little over a litre}

ingredients

200g almonds with skins or
without (water for covering
almonds when soaking)

1 litre cold water

3-4 dates, pitted (optional)

2 tsp sweetener like honey, sugar,
agave syrup, or maple syrup, to
taste (optional)

1 tsp vanilla bean paste (optional)

Preparation time - 30 mins, soaking time - 2 days or overnight

Soak the almonds overnight or up to 2 days with enough water to cover. The longer the almonds soak, the creamier the almond milk will be. Once the time is up, discard the soaking liquid then rinse the almonds throughly under cool running water.

Combine the almonds and a litre of water in a blender.

Blend at the highest speed for 2 minutes then pulse the blender a few times to break up the almonds, (add the dates if using) then blend continuously for two minutes.

The almonds should be broken down into a very fine meal and the water should be white and opaque. (If using a food processor, process for 4 minutes total, pausing to scrape down the sides halfway through.)

Line a strainer with either the opened nut bag or cheese cloth, and place over a tall measuring jug, pour the almond mixture into the strainer.

Press all the almond milk from the almond meal, gather the nut bag or cheese cloth around the almond meal and twist shut.

Squeeze and press with clean hands to extract as much almond milk as possible (Oh, and don't forget to keep your almond pulp on hand! There's no use in wasting any of that goodness…).

Taste the almond milk, and if a sweeter drink is desired, add sweetener to taste together with the vanilla bean paste if required.

Store the almond milk in sealed mason jars in the fridge for up to 2 days.

LISA'S TIP

This almond milk is light enough to serve as a neutral base in smoothies and best of all, it digests seamlessly — unlike conventional dairy, which so many among us (especially those of you who are lactose intolerant) find difficult to stomach. Homemade almond milk only lasts a few days in the fridge; so make just what you think you will drink in this time period. Once kept in the fridge, if the milk separates, just give a gentle stir before serving.

Cashew Butter

Homemade nut butters not only taste better but enable
you to control levels of fat, salt and sugar.

{makes 500g of butter}

ingredients

500g cashew nuts, roasted or raw
(see Lisa's tip for roasting)
2 tsp maple or agave syrup
2-3 pinches sea salt

to serve

serve with gluten-free wholegrain
bread

Preparation time - 15 to 20 mins, cooking time - 13 mins (if you want to roast the cashews)

Add all the cashew nuts to the bowl of your food processor and process for 5 minutes, or until nice and smooth.

At some point, you will have to scrape the sides fairly often, as your nuts will turn into a very thick and crumbly paste.

Although it will take some time and you might think that there's no way your nuts are EVER going to turn into butter – they eventually start to release their oils and turn into nut butter.

Be patient and resist the urge to add any form of liquid.

Just keep going, it will eventually happen! Don't freak when the ball forms, just let it keep going, and you will get nice smooth butter!

From beginning to end, this might take a good 15-20 minutes of active processing, so it is a good idea to give your food processor a few minutes break from time to time.

Just before the end when you reach a consistency you like, add the sea salt and maple or agave syrup.

Keep your nut butter in an air tight container for up to several weeks, if it hasn't been eaten long before then!

LISA'S TIP

You can roast the cashew nuts for approximately 13 minutes, prior to processing, to give that extra nutty flavour. Careful not to burn them! If you want to add a little twist, separate half of the mixture and add 3 tsp Nutella to one half… and give it a quick blend. Now, you can go and grab a spoon!

Coconut Porridge

The addition of coconut water makes this breakfast staple a
little less ordinary – and better for you, too!

{serves 2}

ingredients

570ml coconut water

80g porridge oats fine or rolled

garnish

1 large handful toasted coconut
chips

1 banana

cinnamon

agave syrup

Preparation time - 10 mins, cooking time - 5 mins

Place the coconut water and oats in a non-stick saucepan bring to
boil, stirring often. Simmer for 3 minutes, occasionally stirring.
Leave to sit for 1 minute off the heat.

Toast your coconut chips in a dry frying pan.

Serve with toasted coconut chips, sliced banana, cinnamon and
touch of agave syrup, if required.

LISA'S TIP

*This is a must-try porridge. It's healthy, nutritious, delicious and a
good source of potassium, not just from the banana, but also from
the coconut water, bursting with natural occurring electrolytes. I like
to serve the porridge inside a coconut shell and vary the toppings
to include blueberries, strawberries, chia seeds, or a nice dollop of
cashew butter!*

Heirloom Tomato, Puy Lentil & Halloumi Salad

This is a super simple dish that has a great balance between textures
and flavours – salty halloumi, earthy lentils and sweet, juicy tomatoes.

....

{serves 4}

ingredients

2 heirloom tomatoes, each cut into
4-5 slices

150g cherry tomatoes, cut in half

1 large courgette, julienned with
vegetable peeler (or vegetable spiral
cutter)

¼ red onion, sliced half moons

1 avocado, cubed

100g puy lentils (pre-cooked)

250g halloumi cheese, cut into 10
slices

1 large bunch chopped coriander

2 tbsp olive oil

½ tbsp balsamic vinegar

½ tbsp agave syrup

sea salt and black pepper

garnish

fresh coriander

Preparation time - 40 mins, cooking time - 10 mins

Peel the courgette using a julienne vegetable peeler or spiraliser.

Using a non-stick frying pan, add the halloumi in two batches. Cook
on a medium heat on each side for about 2 minutes until lightly
browned. Place on a plate to cool and drizzle ½ tbsp agave syrup.

In a large mixing bowl add the cherry tomatoes, puy lentils, onion,
coriander, avocado, courgette spirals and season with sea salt and
black pepper.

Toss the salad lightly with 2 tbsp olive oil and ½ tbsp balsamic
vinegar.

On a serving platter, lay out the heirloom tomatoes, place the mixed
salad over the top.

Scatter the halloumi around the salad, and garnish with coriander.

LISA'S TIP

*I always keep halloumi in the fridge since it has a long shelf-life. This
recipe rewards experimentation. Try adding cucumber, pesto, olive
or basil instead of coriander etc. - whatever you fancy. The halloumi
and tomato are robust enough to work brilliantly with a wide variety
of vegetables and herbs. Try spiralising carrots, beetroots, parsnip and
maybe a daikon radish. Get creative!*

Quinoa with Shiitake & Oyster Mushrooms

A tasty side dish or summery main meal.

....

{serves 4-6}

ingredients

225g quinoa, rinsed

450ml cold water

200g fine trimmed green beans, finely chopped

150g shiitake mushrooms, sliced

150g oyster mushrooms, sliced

2 tbsp groundnut oil

1 tbsp sesame oil

4 tbsp soy sauce (gluten-free) or marigold liquid aminos

4 tbsp agave syrup or honey

2 pinches sea salt

garnish

fresh coriander, or flat-leaf parsley

sesame seeds, toasted

Preparation time - 40 mins, cooking time - 20 to 30 mins

Rinse the quinoa, through a fine sieve for about 1 minute.

In a medium saucepan add the quinoa and cold water, bring to a boil then place the lid and simmer on a low light for 20 minutes.

When cooked, remove from the heat and leave to stand for 10 minutes, then lay the quinoa on a large plate to cool down.

Blanch the green beans in boiling salted water for 5 minutes then immerse into cold water to stop the cooking process. Chop finely.

In a large non-stick frying pan, add the groundnut and sesame oil, then the sliced shiitake and oyster mushrooms, sauté until wilted for about 5 minutes, then add the soy and syrup or honey, and simmer for 5 minutes.

Add the cooled quinoa to a large mixing bowl, add the finely chopped green beans and mushrooms, mix all together.

Check for seasoning then garnish with the sesame seeds and coriander.

LISA'S TIP

This quinoa salad with mushrooms and Asian flavours has quickly become one of my new favourite recipes. My relationship with quinoa got off to a rocky start last year but once I gave it another chance and cooked it correctly, I was hooked. High in protein and gluten-free, quinoa is much healthier than white rice/pasta so you don't even need to feel bad about grabbing seconds (or even thirds). Serve with poached eggs for extra protein.

Asian Salmon Fish Cakes

These are time-consuming to make, but the result never fails to please. If you are planning a party, make the fishcakes smaller and top with sweet chilli sauce for an impressive starter.

....

{serves 4 - makes 8 fishcakes}

ingredients

500g fresh salmon fillets, skinned

500g King Edward potatoes, mashed

¼ tsp white peppercorns

1 tbsp white wine (optional)

2 shallots (60g), finely chopped

1 tbsp coconut oil

1 egg yolk

1 ½ tbsp tomato ketchup

1 tsp Dijon or English mustard

2 tsp anchovy essence

1 tbsp sweet chilli sauce

5g coriander, chopped

1 tsp garlic granules

for coating and frying

250g medium cornmeal

2 eggs

corn flour for dusting

250-300ml ground nut (or sunflower) oil

garnish

2 tbsp mayonnaise

1 tbsp sweet chilli sauce

1 tsp ketchup

lemon wedges

rocket

sea salt and white pepper

Preparation time - 60 mins, cooking time - 40 mins

Poach the salmon by placing it in a medium-size pan with enough water to cover, add the white peppercorns and white wine, bring to the boil, then turn off the heat. Cover and leave to stand for 5-10 minutes (depending on the size of the salmon fillets) to cook through. Now remove skin and any grey matter. Separate the salmon into two equal sections and leave to cool.

Take peeled and cut potatoes and place in a medium saucepan. Cover with water and bring to the boil. Cook for 15-20 minutes. Drain, then mash (for best results use a ricer).

Sauté the shallots in the coconut oil, season well with salt and white pepper. In a large mixing bowl, add mashed potato, sautéed shallots, egg yolk, anchovy essence, ketchup, Dijon mustard, sweet chilli sauce and mix. Check for seasoning, you may wish to add a little more of one of the sauces.

Carefully flake one section of the salmon (the salmon will naturally flake) finely and shred the other half. Now add the finely shredded salmon to the potato mixture, then gently fold in the flakes along with the chopped coriander. Lightly dust a large chopping board with corn flour and season with white pepper and sea salt. Shape the mixture into 8 moulds, lightly dust in the flour on both sides then chill in the fridge for 30 minutes. Mix the mayonnaise with the sweet chilli sauce and ketchup for the garnish.

Season the beaten eggs with sea salt, white pepper and garlic granules then dip the fishcakes first into the egg then coat in the cornmeal. Heat 1cm of groundnut oil in a large frying pan (make sure that the oil doesn't get too hot). Fry the fishcakes in two batches for 3-4 minutes each side or until they are golden, crisp and heated through. Drain on a kitchen towel. Serve with rocket and the mayonnaise dip.

LISA'S TIP

You can make these fishcakes in advance and then preheat the oven to 375°F, gas mark 5, 190°C (170°C fan assisted) and heat for 10 minutes, then serve!

Massaged Curly Kale Salad

An unusual dish that has the new 'A-list' vegetable, kale, and
the benefit of creamy avocado and cool green grapes.

{serves 6 - 8}

ingredients

300g fine trimmed green beans,
finely chopped

1 avocado, cubed

200g sliced curly kale (washed),
hard stalks discarded

½ lemon, juice only

2 tbsp extra virgin olive oil

150g green grapes, cut in half
lengthways

50g pistachios, roughly chopped

sesame seeds, handful, toasted

dressing - mint sauce (you will only need half)

10g coriander, fresh

10g mint, fresh

1 garlic clove

100g fat free Greek or soy yogurt
(or coconut milk)

1 tsp agave nectar

1 ripe mango

sea salt and black pepper

garnish

50g pistachios, roughly chopped

1 handful toasted sesame seeds

Preparation time - 30 mins, cooking time - 5 mins

Bring a medium pan of salted water to the boil, cook the fine trimmed green beans for 5 minutes, then drain and run under running cold water, then chop into small pieces, set aside.

To make the dressing, in a blender add the mango, mint, coriander, garlic clove and pulse, then add the yogurt or coconut milk.

Season with sea salt, black pepper and 1 tsp agave nectar.

In a large mixing bowl place the kale add the lemon juice, olive oil and then add sea salt. The salt flavours the kale and also helps soften it by drawing out the water.

Using clean hands, start massaging, keep working the kale until the colour deepens and it feels soft, and tender, this process should take around 2 to 3 minutes.

At this point, stir in the remaining ingredients: avocado, grapes, and beans.

Mix well, cover and allow to sit for an hour before serving to let the flavours meld.

Serve on a large flat platter.

Sprinkle the top with roughly chopped pistachios and toasted sesame seeds.

Drizzle half of the mint dressing over the salad. Keep the remaining dressing in the fridge.

LISA'S TIP

Raw, massaged kale salad is one of my very favourite foods in the entire world – one that would definitely be on my last meal list, and a special friend of mine, Daniel would agree too! The bottom line is, once you learn the massaging technique, which softens the crunchy kale, you'll find yourself improvising versions of this salad left and right! When kale is massaged, its cellulose structure breaks down and wilts, so the leaves that were once tough and fibrous become silky. The kale reduces in volume by over half and the leaves take on a subtle sweetness.

Lamb Chops with Coriander & Mint

Mint is a classic accompaniment to lamb for a reason. Its fresh, cleansing taste is a natural foil to the heavier flavour of the charred meat.

{Serves 2-3}

ingredients

6 lamb cutlets, french trimmed (individual)

marinade

a handful of fresh mint

a handful of fresh coriander

2 cloves garlic

4 tbsp olive oil (a little extra for frying)

2 tbsp sushi seasoning vinegar

2 tbsp sweet chilli sauce

2 tbsp water

1 tbsp soy sauce light

1 tbsp honey

sea salt and black pepper

garnish

fresh coriander, for serving

Preparation time - 20 mins, cooking time - 8 to 10 mins in frying pan or 15 mins in oven

Blitz all the marinade ingredients in a food processor. Taste and adjust sweet/sour/saltiness to perfection.

Place the lamb chops in a food bag and pour in the marinade, tie up and leave to marinate for 4 hours or overnight is best.

Take the chops and marinade out of the bag, pour the sauce in a small saucepan, and gently heat.

Fry the lamb on a medium heat with a little oil, about 7-9 minutes (4 minutes on each side) or more if you prefer it well done; go to a maximum of 10 minutes.

Serve with the sauce drizzled over the cooked lamb chops.

LISA'S TIP

If you prefer you can preheat the oven to 400ºF/ 200ºC (180ºC fan assisted) Gas Mark 6. Heat up a heavy cast iron griddle. Lift the meat out of the marinade, shaking off the excess. Reserving the sauce to heat separately. Sear well on all sides, then transfer to a baking tray and cook in the oven for about 15 minutes, depending how big your cutlets are and how you like your meat cooked. Reduce to 10-12 minutes if you like them pink. I would serve these delicious chops with mange tout, peas and broccoli.

Quinoa Sushi Salad

All the flavours of traditional sushi but in a
salad with beautifully contrasting colours.

....

{Serves 4-6}

ingredients

250g quinoa, rinsed

450ml cold water

2 sweet potatoes

2 tbsp olive oil

4 tbsp sushi seasoning vinegar

3 large eggs, beaten

1 tbsp coconut oil

2 tsp palm sugar

½ cucumber, deseeded and cut into
very small pieces

1 avocado, cut into small cubes

2 nori seaweed sheets, cut into
small strips (best to use kitchen
scissors)

a handful of chives, finely chopped

1 tbsp sesame seeds, toasted

2 tbsp sunflower seeds, toasted

1 tbsp teriyaki or light soy sauce

sea salt and black pepper

garnish

teryaki or soy sauce

Preparation time - 60 mins, cooking time - 30 to 40 mins

Preheat the oven to 350°F, gas mark 4, 180°C (160°C fan-assisted).

Peel and cut the sweet potato into finger size strips.

Place on a baking tray lined with parchment paper, drizzle the olive
oil and season with sea salt and black pepper.

Bake in the preheated oven for 30 minutes, then remove from the
oven to cool.

Place the quinoa in a sieve and rinse under cold running water, for
1 minute.

Then place in a saucepan with 450ml cold water bring to the boil,
then cover and simmer on a low heat for 20 minutes.

After 20 minutes, remove from the heat, carefully fluff with fork,
then leave with the lid on to settle for 10 minutes.

Pour onto a large platter and coat with sushi seasoning vinegar.

In a dry non-stick frying pan toast the sesame and sunflowers seeds
until lightly golden.

To make the omelette beat the eggs season with sea salt, white
pepper and palm sugar.

Melt the coconut oil in a non-stick frying pan and make the
omelette. Place on a plate to cool once cooked.

When the sweet potato and egg have cooled, cut into small cubes.

Add the cooled quinoa to a mixing bowl, add the sweet potato, egg,
cucumber, seaweed, toasted sesame seeds, sunflower seeds, chives
and stir gently till mixed.

Carefully fold in the avocado.

Drizzle over with either teriyaki or soy sauce.

LISA'S TIP

*This lovely salad was created one day, when I had full intentions
of making quinoa sushi. Just as I was about to get rolling I realised
I had run out of nori seaweed sheets. Then I had a flash of
brilliance. SUSHI SALAD! I thought, throw everything together in
a bowl. AMAZING! The resulting salad was tangy, filling, complex,
delicious, and healthy too.*

Chicken Satay Skewers with Spicy Peanut Sauce

This Indonesian dish is a good introduction to Asian cooking
and the use of peanut butter is always surprisingly delicious!

....

{Serves 4-6}

ingredients

500g chicken breast, thinly sliced
into 2.5cm x 5cm slices

8-10 wooden skewers, soaked in
water

marinade

1 tsp ground cinnamon

1 tbsp ground cumin

1 tsp ground black pepper

150ml peanut oil

100ml light soya sauce

2 tbsp palm sugar or agave syrup

spicy peanut sauce

4 tbsp crunchy peanut butter

6 tbsp coconut milk

1 small lime

1 garlic clove, crushed

½ tsp curry powder, mild Madras

2 tsp sweet chilli sauce

1 tsp agave syrup

sea salt and ground white pepper

garnish

½ cucumber, shredded

1 red onion, roughly chopped

baby cos lettuce

handful crushed peanuts

fresh coriander, for serving

lime wedges, for serving

Preparation time - 40 mins, cooking time - 10 to 12 mins (plus 4 hours or overnight marinating)

Put the chicken slices into a bowl and add all marinade ingredients. Stir thoroughly to make sure that all the chicken pieces are coated.

Leave for a minimum of 4 hours in the fridge, preferably overnight, giving it an occasional stir.

Put the coconut milk, peanut butter, and crushed garlic into a saucepan over a gentle heat for about 2 minutes, using a whisk to combine the ingredients together.

Once the peanut butter and coconut milk has combined, remove from the heat.

Squeeze the juice from your lime, and add the curry powder, sweet chilli sauce, agave syrup and salt and pepper into the creamy mixture.

Whisk until smooth, then transfer to a small bowl, cover and set aside until required (the longer you leave it, the more time the flavours will infuse together).

Carefully thread the chicken pieces through the wooden skewers, leaving some space at either end (don't forget that if you are using wooden skewers, soak them in cold water for about 30 minutes before adding the chicken to stop them from burning).

Place the skewers on a hot griddle pan for about 5-6 minutes each side, turning once. Double check that the chicken is cooked through, by testing one piece - you can always grill it for a little longer if necessary.

Serve with chopped raw onion, cucumber shreds, baby cos lettuce, spicy peanut sauce and scattered crushed peanuts.

LISA'S TIP

Serve these straight from the griddle pan or chill and to have at a picnic. These are fun to make with children and can also be cooked on a BBQ. Children always like 'food on a stick'!

Sesame Seared Tuna & Avocado Salsa

This dish has the look of one that has been professionally
prepared, but it is surprisingly easy!

{Serves 4-6}

ingredients

400g tuna loin

1 tbsp black sesame seeds

1 tbsp coconut oil

1 tsp sesame oil

sea salt and black pepper

salsa

2 avocados, chopped

1 red onion, finely chopped

4 medium tomatoes, de-seeded and
chopped

2 tsp sweet chilli sauce

1 lime, cut into wedges

1 tbsp olive oil

dressing

3 spring onions, finely chopped

2 garlic gloves, finely minced

1 lime, juice

2 tbsp fresh coriander

2 tbsp fish sauce

3 tsp palm sugar

2 tbsp honey

1 tbsp sweet chilli sauce

garnish

½ bag of rocket

lime wedges

soy sauce

Preparation time - 60 mins, cooking time - 2 mins, chilling time - 5 to 6 hours or overnight

To make the seared tuna, place the sesame seeds in a shallow tray and season lightly with salt and pepper. Wash and pat dry the tuna lightly with kitchen paper. Using your hands press the tuna into the seasoned sesame seed mixture on all sides. Heat oil in a medium, non-stick sauté pan over medium-high heat and add the coconut and sesame oil. When the oils are very hot, sear the tuna for no longer than 20-30 seconds on each side to seal.

Take the fish off the heat and set aside to rest. When cooled, lay a sheet of cling film on a clean work surface, and then lay another sheet of cling film over the top repeat until you have 4 or 5 layers. Put the tuna at one end of the cling film and roll up tightly to make a fat cigar shape, twist the ends tightly like a cracker (rolling the tuna tightly in cling film will ensure the fish has a good round shape for professional-looking, even slices).

Chill for 5-6 hours – ideally do this in the morning, ready to serve in the evening. For the dressing, mix all the ingredients in a bowl, leave to stand and infuse.

To make the salsa, place the chopped avocado, finely chopped red onion, de-seeded tomatoes, in a bowl with the olive oil, sweet chilli sauce and salt and pepper, toss together.

Half an hour before serving, remove the tuna from the fridge, discard the cling film, then thinly slice. Place equal numbers of slices on each plate. Garnish with avocado salsa in the centre topped with a handful of rocket on each place. Drizzle with dressing on each plate around the tuna, garnish with a lime wedge, serve with a side dish of soy sauce.

LISA'S TIP

When you purchase your tuna, make sure your tuna is shaped like a loin and is bright red or dark pink. If it is maroon or brown, it is not sashimi grade, so it will not be a good candidate for this recipe. **Substitution:** *Beef can be cooked the same way as tuna. For more well done, leave on for 60 seconds on each side.*

Pea Soup

A surprisingly simple but elegant soup.
A few sprigs of fresh dill also works well.

....

{Serves 4-6}

ingredients

1 tbsp olive oil

4 shallots, finely chopped

1 stick of celery, cut in half (will be discarded from the soup before blending)

1 chicken stock cube dissolved in 570ml of boiling water

1 vegetable stock cube dissolved in 570ml of boiling water

1 kilo frozen peas (look for petit pois – the smaller ones)

sea salt and white pepper

garnish

drizzle olive oil

mint

pea shoots

black pepper

Preparation time - 20 mins, cooking time - 20 mins

Finely chop the shallots and cut the celery stalk in half.

Place a saucepan on the stove with the olive oil, sauté the shallots until translucent. Add the celery stalk and season lightly with sea salt and white pepper.

Add the frozen peas and stir for about 2 minutes.

Dissolve the chicken and vegetable stock cubes in a little over a litre of boiling water. Pour into the saucepan, bring to the boil reduce to a medium heat. Cook for 20 minutes.

Remove from the heat, discard the celery stalk and blend either in a liquidiser or with a hand held blender.

Place in individual serving bowls with a drizzle of olive oil for garnish and some pea shoots and mint.

LISA'S TIP

If you find that the soup is too thick after blending, pour in a little water to thin out the soup. Alternatively you can pour the soup through a fine meshed sieve. You may also wish to freeze this soup, for a maximum of 2 -3 months.

Baked Asparagus in Parmesan & Almond Crust

Parmesan is lower in fat than many other cheeses plus its
robust flavour means that a little goes a long way.

{serves 4-6}

ingredients

460g asparagus spears, thick
(approx. 15 spears), trimmed, with
bottom 2/3 of each spear peeled

2 eggs, beaten

2 tsp honey mustard

80g ground almonds

80g parmesan cheese, grated finely

sea salt

white pepper

garlic granules

paprika

avocado dip

2 avocados

2 tsp lemon juice

4 tsp tahini

4 tsp cold water

sea salt & white pepper

Preparation time - 30 mins, cooking time - 20 to 25 mins

Preheat the oven to 425°F, gas mark 7, 220°C (200°C fan assisted).
Line a large baking tray with parchment paper or use a silicon mat.

Cut about 3cm off the bottom of each asparagus, then using a
vegetable peeler, peel halfway down to the bottom of the spear all
around the asparagus, this will eliminate most of the stringiness. It
also looks and tastes better!

In a large oval dish, add the beaten egg, honey mustard, and season
with sea salt, white pepper, garlic granules and paprika. Then soak
the asparagus in the egg mixture, for a minute, then lift out onto a
plate.

Place the ground almonds and grated parmesan on separate plates.

Place one asparagus spear in the egg mixture, then roll in the ground
almonds, then place back in the egg mixture coating all around,
then coat in the parmesan cheese.

When finished coating the asparagus, place on the lined baking tray
and repeat this method with all the asparagus.

If you have extra groud almonds and parmesan, mix together and
sprinkle over the asparagus on the tray.

Place the asparagus in the preheated oven, bake for 20-25 minutes,
turning over after the first ten minutes, and then keep turning over
to ensure all sides are golden and crispy.

To make the dip, in a food processor blend the avocados until
smooth then add the lemon juice, tahini, and water.

Season the dip with sea salt and white pepper and continue to blend
until smooth. Check the seasoning and adjust if needed.

Serve with the avocado dip.

LISA'S TIP

*Make sure the asparagus are not pencil thin. You need thick
asparagus for this recipe. This recipe is suitable for an everyday snack
or served as healthy canapé. Asparagus' season is Spring and, in the
past, I have stir-fried or blanched them. This recipe is easy to make
and tastes great. Mmmm, gorgeous green asparagus dipped into
creamy avocado, nutritious and delicious! Make sure you eat the
crunchy bits which might be left of the tray - they're the best part!*

Tomato Soup

A delicious and healthy soup that lends
itself to making big batches to use later.

....

{makes in excess of 2 litres}

ingredients

1.8kg tomatoes, cut in half
(combination of classic vine, plum,
cherry, Jack Hawkins)

4 enchalion shallots, sliced

2 celery stalks

2 carrots, cut into big batons

2 tbsp olive oil

1 tsp tomato purée

1-2 tsp agave syrup (depending on
the sweetness of the tomatoes, add
2nd spoon if needed after the soup
has been liquidised)

2 tsp bouillon powder

1 litre boiling water

sea salt and black pepper

bouquet garni

garnish

75ml soy cream

2 slices gluten-free brown bread

olive oil

preparation time - 30 mins, cooking time - 40 mins

In a large saucepan add the olive oil and sauté the shallots until
translucent.

Add the tomatoes and continue to sauté for 5 minutes over a
medium heat.

Add the carrots and celery and tomato purée.

Season with sea salt and black pepper.

Add the bouquet garni and agave syrup.

Dissolve the bouillon in the boiling water, then add to tomatoes.

Bring back to a boil then simmer for 40 minutes.

Discard the celery and carrot, before blending.

Blend the soup in a liquidiser in several batches.

Place the sieve over a large bowl and ladle the soup into the sieve.

Using the back of the ladle, push the pulp down into the bowl below.

Continue until all the soup has been sieved and transfer it back into
the pan, reheat if necessary.

To make the croutons, cut both slices of the bread into 1cm cubes,
drizzle with olive oil and sprinkle with sea salt, and bake in the oven
for 8-10 minutes on a medium heat until crisp and browned (watch
they don't burn!).

Taste and adjust seasoning as required.

Stir in the soy cream, sprinkle with black pepper and croutons,
and serve.

LISA'S TIP

*This is one yummy soup. And surprisingly easy. Once you make this,
you'll never be able to go back to canned soups!! This soup improves
on the second day, though it's so good on the first day that there's
often not one drop left. Store it in the refrigerator for 2-3 days, or
freeze it for a couple of months.*

Cauliflower Egg Fried Rice

Ditch the take-away! This delicious dish is low on carbs but features all the flavours of the traditional Chinese dish, without the rice!

{Serves 4}

ingredients

1 large cauliflower (760g approx.), florets broken off

2 echalion shallots, finely chopped

150g frozen petit pois, thawed

3 eggs, beaten

1 tsp sesame oil

1 tbsp coconut oil

sea salt and white pepper

garnish

toasted sesame seeds

teriyaki or soy sauce

Preparation time - 30 mins, cooking time - 20 mins

Break off the cauliflower florets, rinse in a colander and leave to dry completely.

Then place in a food processor until the cauliflower has broken down and you have a rice-like texture (don't over-process or it will get too mushy).

In a mixing bowl, beat the eggs and season with sea salt and white pepper.

In a non-stick frying pan, add the sesame oil, heat and then add the eggs, scramble, then place on a plate when cooked.

In a clean non-stick frying pan, add the coconut oil, sauté the shallots until soft and translucent then season with sea salt and white pepper.

Add the ground cauliflower and cook for 5 minutes, then add the frozen peas and continue to cook for 5 minutes, check for seasoning.

Add the scrambled eggs to the cauliflower and continue to cook.

You can add some teriyaki or soy sauce at this point or leave to garnish.

LISA'S TIP

I LOVE fried rice, and often make my own fried rice at home with brown rice or quinoa which is delicious. But sometimes when I want to cut down on my carbs, I opt for cauliflower rice, an alternative to the typical grain. So tasty, simple and a wonderful way to eat cauliflower.

Crispy Curly Kale

For years this dish has been called 'fried seaweed' in Chinese restaurants.
It's so good, it's hard to believe it's good for you!

{Serves 4}

ingredients

200g curly kale, washed
1-2 tbsp olive oil
sea salt and black pepper
1 tsp coconut sugar

garnish

toasted sesame seeds
onion salad crispies (gluten-free)
½ tsp coconut sugar (if needed)

Preparation time - 5 mins, cooking time - 16 to 18 mins

Preheat the oven to 375°F, gas mark 5, 190°C.

Line a large baking tray with parchment paper.

Place the curly kale on the baking tray and discard any hard stalks.

Drizzle with olive oil, and then lightly massage into the kale leaves.

Season with sea salt and black pepper.

Sprinkle with coconut sugar.

Bake in the preheated oven for 16-18 minutes, stirring every 4-5 minutes.

When the leaves have gone crisp, remove from the oven.

Place in a serving bowl and garnish with toasted sesame seeds, coconut sugar (if needed) and onion salad crispies.

LISA'S TIP

Be sure to check the chips to make sure they don't burn. Kale is now being hailed as the 'queen of greens' since it not only naturally low-calorie, it is packed with Vitamins A and C; A which keeps the eyes healthy, and C, which hydrates the body and speeds up the metabolism. Kale also has powerful antioxidants, including flavonoids and carotenoids.

Lamb Shanks

Serve with creamy polenta or horseradish mashed potatoes. If you want a modern twist you can also serve this dish on a bed on sautéed shallots and edamame beans.

{Serves 4}

ingredients

4 lamb shanks x 275g each, washed and pat dry

250g button mushrooms, finely chopped

300g chantenay carrots, whole

2 small brown onions, peeled and finely chopped

6 shallots, peeled and leave whole

4 garlic cloves, minced

2 x 400g tins cherry tomatoes, sieved, pulp and seeds discarded

2 tablespoons mild acacia honey

3 tablespoons olive oil

570ml chicken stock

50g corn flour

150ml red wine, full-bodied

2 tsp Worcestershire sauce

1 tbsp tomato paste

paprika

sea salt

cracked black pepper

garlic granules

Preparation time - 40 mins, cooking time - 2 ¾ hours

Preheat the oven to 350°F, gas mark 4, 180°C (160°C fan-assisted).

On a chopping board, sprinkle corn flour, paprika, sea salt, cracked black pepper and garlic granules and mix together.

Place each shank in the seasoned flour and coat all side of the shank.

In a large casserole dish, heat the olive oil over a medium heat, place each shank in the casserole dish and brown very well on all sides, then remove from the dish.

Drain away the excess fat in the casserole dish, add the finely chopped onions, mushrooms and garlic, stirring until onions are soft.

Then add the red wine, reduce for 5 minutes, then add the tomato paste.

Place a sieve over the casserole dish and squeeze through tomato sauce, season with garlic granules, sea salt and cracked pepper.

Add the Worcestershire sauce, shallots and carrots.

Return the lamb to the casserole dish, add the chicken stock, bring the liquid to the boil and add the honey.

Cover with a lid and transfer to the oven for 2 ¾ hours, turning lamb shanks occasionally.

After 2 hours reduce the oven temperature to 300°F, gas mark 2, 150°C (130°C fan-assisted) and cook for a further 45 mins.

LISA'S TIP

I have to say I do love meat on the bone and there's something delightful about a braised lamb shank. When the meat is sweet, succulent and soft enough to scrape away with a fork it just can't be beaten. This is a dish I love to serve for family and friends at a dinner party. It's quite a comforting dish and is at its best when its spring lamb!

Asian Fish Stew

This rich, satisfying stew called 'laksa' is a lunchtime treat cooked in Asia's open-air markets. To make the experience truly authentic, be sure to add the beansprouts and lime just before eating!

....

{Serves 4}

ingredients

800g firm, thick white fish fillets (haddock and cod) cut into 5-7cm pieces

450ml fish or chicken stock

sea salt

400ml coconut milk

2 tsp nam pla (Thai fish sauce)

½ tbsp lime juice

250g gluten-free, sweet potato and buckwheat noodles

2 tsp palm sugar

laksa paste

6 coriander stalks with leaves

3 large garlic cloves, crushed

1 fresh red pepper, deseeded and chopped

1 lemon grass stalk, soft centre part only, chopped

3cm piece fresh ginger peeled and chopped

1 tbsp Worcestershire sauce

½ tsp turmeric

2 tbsp groundnut oil

garnish

lime wedges

fresh coriander

55g beansprouts

Preparation time - 30 mins, cooking time - 50 to 60 mins

Put the fish or chicken stock and salt in a saucepan over a high heat and bring slowly to the boil. Then lower the heat and simmer for 10 minutes.

Make the laksa paste by putting put all the remaining paste ingredients (except the oil) in a food processor and blend. Then with the motor running, slowly add up to 2 tbsp of oil until a paste forms.

Heat the oil in a large casserole dish over a high heat, adding the paste and stir-frying until it is fragrant. Now turn off the heat.

Stir the stock into the laksa paste, along with the coconut milk, nam pla, palm sugar and lime juice. Bring to the boil, then lower the heat, cover and simmer for 30 minutes.

Meanwhile, cook the noodles as directed on the packaging until soft. Then run them under cold water. This washes off the starch and stop the cooking. Drain and set aside in a colander.

Add the fish and beansprouts to the simmering laksa stew and continue cooking just until the fish is cooked through, approx. 10 minutes.

Pour boiling water over the noodles to refresh them. Divide the noodles between four bowls and ladle to stew over, making sure everyone gets an equal share of the fish.

Garnish with the beansprouts, lime wedges and coriander.

LISA'S TIP

You can substitute the fish with chicken, tofu, mushrooms or combine them all. This is one of the most requested recipes for a get-together with my friends. Maybe it's because the sweet, sour, spicy, salty and savoury flavours of Asia are a fantastic way to fill a bowl. And this is also an easy dish to make. Try potato & buckwheat, soba or black rice noodles for variety.

Sticky BBQ Chicken

This Sticky BBQ Chicken can be made year-round in the oven.
Serve crunchy salads to accompany.

....

{Serves 4-6}

ingredients

8 x chicken thighs, skin-on and bone-in

1 tbsp sesame oil

garlic granules

paprika

sea salt and white pepper

marinade

½ lemon, juice

2 celery stalks, peeled (stringy bits removed) and grated on a microplane

2 enchalion shallots, grated on a microplane

2 garlic cloves, crushed

1 tsp ginger, minced

100ml tomato pasta sauce (a smooth sauce is best)

50ml cold water

50ml soy sauce

50ml mirin sweet rice vinegar

2 tsp American mustard

2 tsp sweet chili sauce

3 tsp acacia honey

Preparation time - 40 mins, cooking time - 50 to 60 mins

Preheat the oven to 400°F, gas mark 6, 200°C, (180°C fan-assisted).

Mix all ingredients for marinade in a large mixing bowl (keep 100ml aside for heating up in a sauce pan to serve).

Rub the sesame oil into the chicken thighs, and season well with white pepper, garlic granules, sea salt and paprika.

Place the thighs in large sealable bags, spoon over some over the marinade to cover the thighs and let marinate for 10–15 minutes or preferably overnight.

When ready to cook, remove thighs and reserve marinade.

Transfer the chicken into a roasting tray with a couple of spoonfuls of marinade.

Place in the oven for about 50-60 minutes, turning occasionally and basting with the marinade and juices until thoroughly sticky and golden, adding extra marinade to the tray if necessary.

Start basting the thighs after 20 minutes and then baste 2 or 3 times for the duration of the cooking process.

They'll be done when they are nicely browned and the juices run clear when pierced with a knife (it's important you cook the chicken all the way through).

Heat reserved marinade in a small saucepan, reduce heat and simmer 5 minutes.

Once the chicken pieces are cooked, eat them when fresh and hot. Just before serving, pour some extra sauce over them or leave to cool before packing up for a picnic or packed lunch.

LISA'S TIP

If you would prefer to you can cook these thighs on the BBQ. Note that sauces with high sugar content will cause flare-ups when cooking over direct heat and may burn the chicken. Where possible apply BBQ sauce towards the end of the grilling time - just enough for the sauce to caramelize and crust on the chicken without burning. You can use the extra sauce to marinate lamb chops, too.

Shoulder of Lamb Baked with Rice

Sweet raisins and cinnamon give this
classic lamb stew a Middle Eastern twist.

{Serves 6-8}

ingredients

1 kg shoulder of lamb, cubed

500g red rice, rinsed

500ml cold water

2 red onions, finely chopped

2 echalion shallots, finely chopped

150g puy lentils, ready-to-eat (pre
cooked)

100g sultanas

350ml passata sauce

4 tbsp coconut oil

2 garlic cloves, crushed

2 handfuls coriander, chopped

300ml almond milk

1 tbsp honey

sea salt, white pepper and black
pepper

garlic granules

paprika

cinnamon

garnish

2 tbsp coconut oil

2 brown onions, sliced

150g toasted cashew nuts

coriander

Preparation time - 1 hour, cooking time - 2 hours

Preheat the oven to 400°F, gas mark 6, 200°C (180°C fan-assisted).

Rinse the red rice, then place in a saucepan with 500ml cold water, bring to boil then simmer for 30 minutes. Remove from heat, fluff with a fork, and leave covered for a further 10 minutes. Place a large non-stick frying pan over a medium heat, add the cubed lamb and cook until you release all the juices.

Brown the lamb (you may need to pour away the juices every so often) this can take 5-10 minutes. In a large mixing bowl add: sea salt, white pepper, black pepper, garlic granules, paprika and cinnamon. Add the browned lamb to the seasoning, coat and marinate for 10 minutes.

In a large 29cm oven-proof casserole dish, add 2 tbsp coconut oil and sauté the shallots until soft, then add the cooked rice and continue to cook for 1 minute. Remove half of the rice mixture out of the casserole dish and set aside. With the back of a large spoon, smooth out the rice in the casserole dish on the base, and then spread equally 2 inches around the sides of the dish. Set aside.

Add 1 tbsp coconut oil to a large non-stick frying pan, sauté the red onions until translucent, add garlic, coriander, puy lentils, raisins, tomato sauce and honey and cook for further 10 minutes. Add the almond milk, bring to the boil, then simmer and add the lamb. Cook for 5 minutes. Carefully spoon the lamb and sauce into the prepared rice dish. Now evenly cover with the remaining rice and smooth out with the back of the spoon. Place in the preheated oven and cook covered for 1.5 hours.

For the last 30 minutes remove the lid and decrease the oven temperature to 350°F, gas mark 4, 180°C (160°C fan-assisted). In a small saucepan add 2 tbsp coconut oil and fry the sliced onions until crispy. Place on paper towel and sprinkle with sea salt. Roast the cashew nuts in the oven for 10-12 minutes until browned. When you're ready to serve, scatter onions, cashew nuts and coriander.

LISA'S TIP

This is a delicious one pot wonder dish. It's light, delicate and rich in flavours. It is perfectly accompanied by some chutneys and pickles and a light green salad.

Oven Baked Cod with Peppers & Olives

In Mediterranean coastal towns, the cuisine often combines the acidic flavour of tomatoes and fresh fish. With healthy dishes like this, no wonder their diet is considered the best!

{serves 4}

ingredients

4 x 200g cod fillets, skinless (middle pieces)

100ml extra virgin olive oil, plus extra for drizzling

1 garlic clove, crushed with salt to a puree

2 red onions, finely sliced

2 red peppers, skins removed, deseeded and thinly sliced

2 yellow peppers, skins removed, deseeded and thinly sliced

60g black olives, pitted (Nicoise or Kalamata)

2 tsp capers (optional)

salt and freshly ground black pepper

10g coconut oil

tomato sauce

1 box of baby tomatoes

4 shallots

2 garlic cloves,

2 tbsp brandy (optional)

2 tsp tomato paste

400ml chicken or vegetable stock

1 tbsp agave nectar or honey

400g vine tomatoes, deseeded or you can use canned

1 bouquet garni (bay leaf, celery, thyme, leek) small pieces

50g coconut oil

1 tbsp olive oil

mixed herbs

garnish

Greek basil

Preparation time - 1 hour, cooking time - stove 30 mins, oven 8 to 10 mins

To peel the peppers, place them whole under a preheated grill until they blacken, turning occasionally, about 10-12 minutes.

Remove from the grill and place in a large bowl and cover with cling wrap (or a food bag) until the peppers cool. Then deseed and thinly slice.

For the tomato sauce, slice the shallots, fry until soft with a little olive oil in a saucepan.

Add the chopped garlic, being careful not to burn the garlic, then add the tomato paste.

Cut the tomatoes in half and deseed, alternatively you may wish to use canned tomatoes. Add to the saucepan together with the baby tomatoes.

Add 200ml of chicken stock. Turn the heat up until the sauce begins to boil, then reduce the temperature, season with salt and pepper, add bouquet garni and a sprinkle of mixed herbs.

Slowly add the remaining stock, add cartouche (parchment paper pan lid with hole in the middle to let the steam out). Simmer slowly for 20 mins.

Pour sauce ingredients through a fine sieve, return to stove on a low heat and gradually add honey or agave syrup and brandy. Slowly whisk in the coconut oil, then leave to the side.

Heat a little oil in a large heavy-based frying pan, add the red onions and sauté until soft about 6 minutes. Then add the garlic, olives and peppers, cook for a further 2 minutes seasoning lightly with a little salt and pepper. Add tomato sauce and capers, if using.

Preheat oven to gas mark 5, 190°C, (170°C fan-assisted).

Warm sauce over a medium /heat.

In an oven proof dish pour in your tomato sauce, then add the cod to the ovenproof dish.

Cook for approximately 8-10 minutes.

Garnish with fresh springs of Greek basil or fresh oregano.

LISA'S TIP

If you are short for time you can skip the process of making your own tomato sauce and use a good quality smooth pasta sauce. You could serve this with some gluten-free bread or a side dish of either polenta, quinoa or brown rice.

Beef with Asparagus and Teriyaki Sauce

This is a lighter version than the one found in restaurants. There's no MSG or flour and the oil has been minimised. Try serving the dish with Cauliflower Fried Rice.

{serves 4}

ingredients

2 tbsp groundnut oil

500g beef rump or sirloin steak, sliced thinly

1 large brown onion, sliced thinly

340g asparagus, trimmed, peeled and cut into 3 pieces diagonally

3 spring onions, cut into 3cm slices

2 cloves of garlic, crushed

1 tbsp palm sugar

2 tbsp teriyaki sauce

2 tbsp soy sauce

1 tbsp water

1 tsp grated ginger

1 tsp sesame oil

garnish

2 tbsp roasted cashew nuts

1 small chilli, sliced (optional for garnish)

bunch of fresh coriander

brown rice

Preparation time - 40 mins, cooking time - 15 to 20 mins

Prepare your asparagus by taking the root end off and, using a vegetable peeler, remove the top layer off around the asparagus 2.5cm from the bottom of the tip. Then cut into 3 pieces diagonally.

Now prepare your spring onions cutting them into 3cm slices.

Slice the beef in 1.5cm strips across the length of the piece.

Heat half the oil in a wok, stir fry the beef in batches until browned, then transfer to a plate to rest.

Mix the teryaki sauce, soy sauce, sugar and 1 tbsp water, then set aside.

Heat the remaining oil in the wok and stir fry the onion until soft and translucent, then add the asparagus and continue cooking for 10-12 minutes until al dente.

Return the beef to the wok with the garlic and ginger and cook for 30 seconds.

Add the spring onions, stir fry for 2 minutes, then add the sauce and cook for a further minute.

Drizzle with the sesame oil, then scatter with cashew nuts and sliced chilli (optional) and garnish with coriander.

Serve immediately with steamed brown rice or gluten-free noodles.

LISA'S TIP

Asparagus - long regarded as one of the 'foods of love' is back! Asparagus is available from different parts of the world all year round, but British asparagus is well worth waiting for – it has unbeatable flavour and freshness. The tips should be tightly furled and perky, rather than limp, and the shoots should be straight and firm.

Banana & Peanut Butter Ice Cream Cake

Both bananas and peanuts have positive health properties,
so here's a way of having your cake and eating it too!

{serves 8 - 10}

ingredients

200g crunchy granola bars, crushed

2 tbsp coconut oil, melted

8 bananas, cut into 3cm pieces, and put into the freezer

100ml soya single cream

4 tbsp crunchy peanut butter

garnish

50g dark chocolate, melted

Preparation time - 30 mins, freezing time - 6 to 8 hours or overnight for finished cake to set and allow time to pre-freeze banana chunks

Remove bananas from skins, cut into 3cm cubes and freeze until hard.

Line a 9 inch (23cm) loose bottomed, round cake tin with parchment paper.

Place the granola bars in a food processor and pulse until sandy consistency.

Melt the coconut oil over a gentle heat, then add the crushed granola bars.

Place the biscuit mixture into the prepared tin, press firmly into the base and 3cm around the sides.

Place the banana slices in a food processor or powerful blender.

Purée banana slices, scraping down the bowl as needed.

Purée until the mixture is creamy and smooth, then add the soya single cream.

Add the crunchy peanut butter and purée to combine, then pour the mixture into the cake tin and freeze for 6-8 hours or overnight.

30 minutes before you are ready to serve, remove ice cream cake from the freezer.

Melt the dark chocolate and drizzle over the cake.

Smile.

LISA'S TIP

If you are looking for a new way to use up your ripe bananas, try this Banana Peanut Butter Ice Cream cake. I always have loads of frozen banana chunks in my freezer, whether it's for a smoothie or this delicious cake. The recipe is super simple to make and no one will ever know there are only a few ingredients involved. This recipe really is magical, and healthy too!

Lemon & Almond Cake

A fine textured cake which
is very rich – so small slices!

....

{serves 10}

ingredients

175g butter, room temperature

175g coconut sugar

100g fine cornmeal

1 tsp baking powder

175g ground almonds, sifted

1 unwaxed lemon, grated and freshly squeezed

½ tsp vanilla extract

3 medium eggs

drizzle

2 unwaxed lemons, grated and freshly squeezed

50g icing sugar

2 tbsp water

Preparation time - 30 mins, cooking time - 30 mins, cooling time 20 mins

Preheat the oven to 350°F, gas mark 4, 180°C (160°C fan-assisted).

Cream together the butter and sugar, add the eggs and vanilla extract and beat until roughly blended (do not over-beat as you do not want to incorporate too much air).

Add the fine cornmeal, baking powder, ground almonds, and if you are using a food processor make sure you wipe the sides of the bowl during the mixing.

And the juice and zest of one lemon, and mix together until smooth.

Line the base of a non-stick 20cm springform cake tin with parchment paper, spoon the mixture in, level out and bake in the middle of the preheated oven for 30 minutes.

To make the syrup drizzle, place the lemon zest and juice in a small saucepan together with the icing sugar and water bring to a boil for 2-3 minutes then reduce to a simmer for 3 minutes to reduce the consistency to a syrup.

After 30 minutes remove the cake from the oven, let it cool on a wire rack for 5 minutes.

Pierce the cake with a fine skewer or tooth pick making a about 20 small holes.

Pour the syrup through a sieve into a small bowl, then using a large spoon carefully pour the syrup over the cake (keep the rind as a garnish).

Loosen the springform tin and leave for 20 minutes while the cake absorbs the syrup.

Release the cake from the tin, and serve.

LISA'S TIP

This recipe does have sugar and butter, although that's why it's in my treats section. I love the richness, moistness and lemony punch that this cake delivers! It is the ideal dessert for a glorious afternoon tea and would also make a scrummy pudding with a big dollop of frozen lemon curd sorbet!

Almond Macaroons

Different from macarons which are two lids with a filling, these macaroons
are the traditional ones made by grandmothers everywhere!

{Makes 20 macaroons}

ingredients

225g ground almonds
2 large eggs, whites onlt
115g coconut sugar
20 almonds, whole blanched

Preparation time - 20 mins, cooking time - 18 to 20 mins

Preheat the oven to 325°F, gas mark 4, 180°C (160°C fan assisted)

In a large mixing bowl add the ground almonds and coconut sugar and mix well.

Gradually pour in the egg whites, then mix well to form a sticky mixture.

Pre line a large baking tray with greaseproof paper.

Roll a heaped teaspoon of the almond mixture in the palm of your hands into a ball, (I wet my hands slightly to prevent too much sticking!). Then place on the tray 4 rows of 5 spacing them evenly.

Dip your finger in a small bowl filled with cold water, flatten slightly then gently press into the macaroon and place a blanched almond in the middle.

Place in the pre-heated oven on the middle shelf for 18-20 minutes.

Allow to cool, then place on a wire rack to cool.

LISA'S TIP

These are a great treat if you're following a gluten/dairy free diet! They are my grandma's special recipe and we make them together. The tip with macaroons is that they bake quickly and it's a judgement call as to when they are done enough. I actually prefer the pale ones which are soft throughout, although some people prefer a little colour and a harder shell. To be honest they taste great pale or slightly browned, and if they last longer than a day (highly unlikely), they will get firmer in time so I would lean towards a light brown colour. They are great with a cup of tea or coffee any time!

Banana & Walnut Cake

A light textured cake with rich frosting – just make sure to have friends and family around so you can share!

{Serves 12 - 14}

ingredients

3 large eggs
200ml sunflower oil
3 bananas, mashed
225g coconut sugar, sifted
225g fine cornmeal (polenta), sifted
1 pinch sea salt
2 tsp baking powder
100g walnuts, broken up
100g sultanas

garnish

220g Philadelphia (or other full-fat) cream cheese
80g slightly salted butter
2 tsp custard powder
4 tbsp icing sugar
60g walnuts halves

Preparation time - 40 mins, cooking time - 55 mins, decorating time - 20 mins

Preheat the oven to 325°F, gas mark 3, 160°C, (140°C fan-assisted).

In a food mixer, or by hand, beat the eggs. Then add the sunflower oil.

In a large mixing bowl sift the sugar, cornmeal, baking powder and salt, then add to the egg mixture. Beat until combined.

Fold in the mashed bananas, then add the broken walnuts and sultanas.

Line the base and sides of a non-stick 9in (23cm) spring form tin with parchment paper.

Pour in the mixture and bake on the middle shelf of the preheated oven for 55 minutes.

Remove from the oven when cooked and place on a cooling rack. After ten minutes, release the spring form tin and leave to cool.

To make the cream cheese frosting, beat by hand the cream cheese and butter until smooth. Add the custard powder and icing sugar.

When the cake is cooled, ice the cake, sides and top and decorate with walnut halves.

Remember to share!

LISA'S TIP

Okay, the recipe has sugar but I've balanced this out by making the recipe gluten-free. It truly is like banana bread in a fluffier form. Bananas have always been one of my favourite fruits for breakfasts and snacks and I love walnuts which are good for our brain and memory. So, I tried different experiments with both ingredients and the result is addictive! And, as bananas are packed full of goodness, including Vitamin C, potassium and dietary fibre. Any cake baked with them are my family's favourite, especially my grandma.

SUMMER

seasonal moods

Heat. Yes, even here. Where thoughts drift to recreating dishes we've had on holiday. Where we can stand outside and barbecue (even if we sometimes need an umbrella) fish or kebabs of fresh vegetables - all accompanied by giant salads with the rich red hues of tomatoes, brilliant gold of corn on the cob, creamy green of avocados, cucumbers and the more exotic edamame bean.

Then there are strawberries enjoyed on their own or with their seasonal friend, blueberries. Perhaps adding a dash of Middle Eastern mystery - dates.

It is an easy time to eat foods that are light and healthy. Choices are plentiful so get chopping.

AVOCADO Delicious and creamy, avocados provide nearly 20 essential nutrients, including fibre, potassium, vitamin E, B vitamins and folic acid.

CUCUMBER Containing more than 96% water and in the same family as melons and squashes, cucumbers are easily grown in many climates and are found in most global cuisines.

DATES Used in recipes instead of refined sugar, fresh dates should be plump and moist with glossy skins. Dried dates should still be glossy with an even colour.

STRAWBERRIES You may not realise that strawberries are actually part of the rose family and not technically a fruit. Low in sugar, they are ideal for people following a low-GI diet.

TOMATOES Forget oranges - tomatoes pack a mega punch when it comes to vitamin C. They also contain vitamin A, energy-boosting iron and potassium, which has been proven to reduce strokes.

BLACKBERRIES As well as tasting wonderful, blackberries are also rich in vitamins, minerals and antioxidants. They are also low in calories, carbohydrates and fat, making them one of the best fruits out there for a balanced diet.

BROCCOLI A close relative of cauliflower, and from the same family as cabbage and sprouts, broccoli has grown wild in the Mediterranean for hundreds of years.

EDAMAME BEANS Edamame are young soybeans usually still in the pod. The beans are picked when they are young and green ensuring they are soft and edible. Edamame are prized among vegetarians for their high protein content.

Berry & Oat Smoothie Bowl

People on gluten-free diets sometimes struggle at breakfast. Here's one solution that is a cross between oatmeal and a classic smoothie. Be sure to include the toppings for variety.

{serves 4-6}

ingredients

500ml almond milk

160g frozen berries (strawberries, blueberries, raspberries and blackberries)

2 tsp agave nectar (optional)

20g gluten-free oats

2 large bananas, fresh or frozen

garnish

banana chips, broken up

granola, gluten-free

blueberries

raspberries

blackberries

Preparation time - 20 mins, freezing fruits 6 - 8 hours

Peel and slice your bananas if not already frozen.

In a blender, combine the almond milk, bananas, frozen berries and agave nectar.

Process until the mixture is smooth.

Add the oats and give a quick pulse.

Divide between two breakfast bowls and top with banana chips, granola, blueberries, raspberries and blackberries.

Enjoy with a clear conscience!

LISA'S TIP

This smoothie is perfect for a 'get up and go' morning. What's even better is that you can make it the night before and let it sit in the fridge. It will naturally thicken overnight that's why I like to serve it as a smoothie bowl rather than in a glass. For added fibre, I like to add some chia seeds or shredded toasted coconut, pecans, hemp seeds, cashew butter, fresh banana slices and strawberries and blueberries.

Freezing is the easiest and cheapest way to preserve fresh fruit and prevent food wastage. When I shop, I make sure to buy a good selection of fruit at different states of ripeness. I buy riper fruit to eat at the beginning of the week, and unripe fruit to eat later in the week. When I end up with too much ripe fruit at one time, I freeze the excess to use in smoothies and other foods!

Scrambled Eggs with Smoked Salmon & Avocado

Creamy scrambled eggs with flavourful salmon, a brunch
classic that also makes a quick and tasty dinner.

....

{serves 4}

ingredients

10-12 large eggs, beaten (I like to
use 3 eggs person, however you can
choose 2 per person)

sea salt

white pepper

black pepper

2 tbsp coconut oil

garnish

2 avocados, sliced and seasoned
with salt and black pepper

227g smoked salmon

chives

gluten-free wholemeal bread

Preparation time - 15 mins, cooking time - 3 to 5 mins

Break the eggs into a bowl and lightly beat them, season with sea
salt and white pepper.

Melt the coconut oil in a large non-stick pan on a high heat, then
add the eggs and reduce the heat to low.

Keep on the low heat, stirring continuously with a wooden spoon.
Continuously stirring over a low heat keeps the eggs nice and
creamy with the help of the coconut oil.

The eggs must remain soft and creamy, so keep a eye on them.

Always remove scrambled eggs from the heat when they are almost
set but still appear shiny and a bit underdone, as they carry on
cooking in the pan.

If it is necessary to hold scrambled eggs for a short time before
serving (while putting on the toast!) take off the direct heat earlier.

Cut the avocados in half, make slices across the length. Scoop out of
the skin and season with sea salt and black pepper.

Just before serving you can chop up some chives for presentation
and serve with the smoked salmon and avocado.

Enjoy with friends.

LISA'S TIP

*Good scrambled eggs can be tricky to make because the mistake so
many people make is turning the heat up higher than necessary to
make them cook quicker. This will make them cook quicker – but it
will also make them rubbery. So be patient and always keep the heat
on medium/low, it is worth it for a decent result.*

Chia Seed & Granola Individual Breakfast Pots

By placing the mixture in Mason jars, you have now portioned for
four breakfasts. Little things like this help to de-stress our lives.

{makes 4 individual pots}

ingredients

500ml almond milk
8 tbsp chia seeds
2 tbsp agave nectar
240g gluten-free granola
100g blueberries
100g raspberries
100g blackberries

garnish

4 strawberries
agave syrup for drizzling

Preparation time - 30 mins, refrigeration 6 to 8 hours (overnight)

Pour 500ml almond milk into a measuring cup and add the agave
syrup and chia seeds. Give it a mix and then ten minutes later give
it another stir, cover with cling film and then leave either overnight
or for at least a few hours.

Wash and pat dry your berries.

Remove the chia seed pudding from the refrigerator and give a
gentle stir.

Using 4 Mason type jars with lids, layer the jars with chia seed
pudding at the bottom then berries, granola then repeat with chia
seed pudding, berries and granola.

Garnish with strawberries and a drizzle of agave syrup. Either eat
straight away for a scrummy filling breakfast on the move (it travels
well) or as a snack or dessert.

Keep in the refrigerator for 2 to 3 days once made.

Just as great with a variety of fruits!

LISA'S TIP

*Now I love a good chia pudding, especially for breakfast or dessert.
In fact anytime of the day! If you have your ear to the health-food
ground, then you've heard of chia seeds, superfood extraordinaire.
Packed with great things; full of fibre, healthy fatty acid omega 3,
very high in protein and full of vitamins, these unassuming seeds are
more than meets the eye.*

Tomato & White Peach Salad

White peaches have a short season
so grab them when you see them!

{serves 4}

ingredients

6 large tomatoes, skinned and de-seeded

3 white peaches, each cut into 12 slices

125g goats cheese soft & creamy

6 basil leaves, sliced thinly

1 handful chives, chopped

2 tbsp extra virgin olive oil

2 tbsp toasted pine nuts

1 tbsp pumpkin seeds

1-2 tsp agave nectar

sea salt and

black pepper

garnish

a few basil leaves scattered

red garnet micro herb

Preparation time - 30 mins, cooking time - 5 mins

To remove skin from tomatoes, bring a large pan of water to the boil, and have a large bowl filled with ice cold water on the side. Cut a very shallow X on the top and bottom and drop them into the boiling water 3 at a time. Using a slotted spoon, remove the tomatoes after 20-30 seconds and place into the prepared bowl of ice water. Let the tomatoes sit for at least 5 minutes.

Once the tomatoes have been chilled, remove, then peel. If the skin is stubborn, use a small sharp paring knife being careful not to squeeze the tomato. Once skinned, cut each tomato into quarters, then use a small knife or a teaspoon and scoop the seeds out. Now cut each quarter in half and place in a large mixing bowl. Season with sea salt and black pepper. Add extra virgin olive oil, chopped chives, sliced basil and mix well.

Remove the peach stone by cutting the peach in half, and then cut each half into 6 slices. Add to the tomatoes.

Toast the pine nuts in a non-stick dry frying pan over a medium heat, keep shaking to prevent burning, place in a small bowl and add the pumpkin seeds.

To serve, place the tomatoes and peaches on a large platter, scatter the pine nuts, pumpkin seeds and goats cheese. Drizzle the agave nectar, garnish with basil sprigs and red garnet microherb.

LISA'S TIP

Savoury peach dishes aren't usually the first to come to mind but they are a fruit that goes beautifully with many cheeses and herbs.

Avocado, Cherry Tomato & Pine Nut Salad

Chock full of fresh herbs, this easily composed salad is
made special by the addition of pine nuts.

....

{serves 4 -6}

ingredients

440g cherry tomatoes, cut in half
220g trimmed fine beans
35g toasted pine nuts
1 bunch coriander, finely chopped
1 bunch mint, finely chopped
1 bundle chives, finely chopped
2 avocados, each half sliced into 5
3 tbsp extra virgin olive oil
½ tbsp lemon juice
sea salt
black pepper

garnish

fresh coriander
balsamic glaze

Preparation time - 20 mins, cooking time - 5 mins

Place the beans into boiling salted water and cook for 5 minutes. Then immediately place in a sieve and run under cold water to stop the cooking process. Now chop the beans finely.

Toast the pine nuts in a dry pan for 3-5 minutes, continually shaking the pan to prevent burning.

In large mixing bowl, add the cherry tomatoes which have been cut in half, chopped herbs, pine nuts and green beans. Toss well.

In a small bowl, mix the olive oil and lemon juice and season with sea salt and black pepper. Pour over the tomatoes.

Place the salad on your serving plates.

Then carefully place the sliced avocado over the salad.

Check for seasoning, garnish with balsamic glaze and coriander!

LISA'S TIP

This salad is simple and delicious. It's a great way to make use of the summer bounty of tomatoes. Enjoy as a starter or side dish or copy me and eat it as your main meal. This salad is packed with nutrition. It complements fish, meat and poultry if serving as a side dish.

Lemon and Rosemary Chicken

Easy to prepare and bursting with citrus flavour.
Serve with Pan-Fried Jersey Royal Potatoes.

{serves 4}

ingredients

4 chicken breast (supreme on the bone with skin)
2 whole garlic bulbs
1 lemon, large
2 tbsp olive oil
sea salt and cracked black pepper
garlic granules
2 stalks of rosemary

Preparation time - 30 mins, cooking time - 40 mins (If you have time you can marinate for 2 hours or overnight)

Pre-heat the oven to 350°F, gas mark 4, 180°C (160°C fan-assisted).

Place the chicken breast in a hot frying pan with a little olive oil to seal the chicken, 2 minutes each side until the skin is crisp and golden, then place in your roasting dish.

Cut both garlic bulbs in half, then rub all over the chicken breast and place in the middle of the roasting dish.

Season with salt, black pepper and garlic granules on either side.

Slice your lemon into 6 slices, and place over the chicken and squeeze each of the leftover ends over the chicken.

Scatter 2 stalks of rosemary around the baking dish. Don't worry about the rosemary sticking to the chicken, it tastes great when it's cooked.

Pour a generous amount of olive oil - around 2 tablespoons - over the chicken.

Place in the oven for 40 minutes, turning over after the first 20 minutes, start with the skin side down.

Cut your chicken breast in half on the diagonal when serving.

LISA'S TIP

These chicken breast are full of flavour and simple, yet fancy enough for your next summer garden party. Grilled chicken breast is one of my favourites. It is lean, tender and juicy. I love how the lemon slices caramelizes during the cooking and becomes sweeter. .

Red Quinoa & Greek Feta Salad

Adding red quinoa to this Greek inspired salad makes the dish a more substantial one – meaning to less desire to snack in the afternoon!

{serves 4}

ingredients

250g red quinoa

350ml cold water

1 large cucumber, (peeled and deseeded) cut in small slices

250g medium size tomatoes, (deseeded) cut in half or quarters

200g feta cheese, crumbled

60g Kalamata or green olives, sliced in half lengthways

¼ red onion, finely chopped

sea salt or herbamare and black pepper

dressing

60ml extra virgin olive oil

4 tsp sushi seasoning vinegar

2 tsp Dijon honey mustard

2 tsp balsamic vinegar

garnish

fresh mint

Preparation time - 40 mins, cooking time - 30 mins

Place the quinoa in a sieve and rinse under cold running water, drain and then place in a medium-size saucepan with 350ml cold water. Bring to a boil then simmer for 20 minutes with the lid on.

After 20 minutes, remove from the heat, carefully fluff with a fork and leave to stand for ten minutes. Then place on a large plate to cool.

Remove the skin of the cucumber with a vegetable peeler. Cut down the length in half then each half again, then run the blade of your knife under the base of the seeds down the length of the cucumber, removing them.

Slice each quarter of the cucumber into smaller slices, then place in a large mixing bowl.

Cut the tomatoes in half, remove the seeds then cut in half again, add to the mixing bowl.

Add the sliced olives and red onion to the cucumber and tomatoes and season well with sea salt and black pepper.

In a separate bowl, make the dressing by whisking the olive oil, Dijon honey mustard, sushi seasoning and balsamic vinegar.

Fold the cooled red quinoa into the salad, toss, then drizzle over the dressing.

Add the crumbled feta and check for seasoning.

Garnish with fresh mint and serve.

LISA'S TIP

Just before serving I like to add in some avocado, to give a little creamy texture, you can also add some sundried tomatoes, or artichokes. For those who do not know, quinoa is a type of edible seed that originated in the Andes of South America. Quinoa is pronounced 'keen-wah' and not 'key-nowah' like I first thought!

Seared Steak, White & Green Bean Salad

Will convert even the most stalwart of 'meat and potatoes' men!
My father has just asked for me to make it again!

....

{serves 4-6}

ingredients

4 sirloin or rump steaks

300g cherry tomatoes, cut in half (combination of yellow and red cherry tomatoes)

300g French green beans, blanched

4 large tomatoes, skinned & de-seeded

410g white butter beans, tinned, rinsed and drained

1 tbsp coconut oil

sea salt and black pepper

garlic granules

paprika

dressing

2 shallots, finely chopped

2 handfuls basil

2 handfuls coriander

2 tbsp sushi seasoning vinegar

1 tbsp sweet chilli sauce

100ml extra virgin olive oil, plus 2 tbsp olive oil for frying shallots

1 tsp agave syrup

2 garlic cloves

garnish

½ red onion sliced

crispy fried onions, salad toppers (gluten-free)

Preparation time - 40 mins, cooking time - 10 mins

Cook the beans in slightly salted water for 4-5 minutes, take out using a slotted spoon (retaining salted water on the stove), immerse beans in cold water to stop the cooking process, then drain.

Using the same water as above make a cross incision on the top of the tomatoes, then place in the boiling water for 2 minutes, then into cold water to remove the skins, when cooled, cut into quarters and de-seed, then cut into strips.

Drain the butter beans through a sieve and place in a large mixing bowl, add the cherry tomatoes, larger tomato strips and green beans.

To make the dressing, finely chop the shallots, fry in 2 tbsp olive oil until sautéed and then add the garlic. Season with sea salt and black pepper.

Place the shallots and garlic in a mixing bowl and leave to cool.

In a mini chopper, place the cooled shallots and garlic, the remaining olive oil, vinegar, sweet chilli sauce, agave syrup and chopped herbs. Blend and then taste for seasoning.

Pour half of this dressing into the bowl with the tomatoes and beans. Toss, then place on a flat serving platter.

Season the steaks on both sides with sea salt, black pepper, garlic granules and paprika.

Heat a non-stick frying with 1 tbsp coconut oil, cook the steaks over a medium/high heat for 2-3 minutes per side or until cooked to your liking.

Remove, place on a plate and leave to rest (the steaks will continue cooking while resting, so don't overcook if you like it pink).

Slice the steak into equal size strips, and place over the beans and tomatoes.

Drizzle with the remaining dressing.

Garnish with the sliced red onion and crispy fried onions.

LISA'S TIP

This delicious steak salad has a fiesta of flavours, for a quick and tasty family friendly weeknight meal. I am currently in tomato heaven! Tomatoes are in season and I am love, love, loving them! Tomatoes combined with the hearty white and string beans and tossed with this mouthwatering dressing is a knockout combination!

Quinoa Salmon & Avocado Sushi

Don't worry if your first sushi rolls
aren't perfect – it takes practice!

{serves 4}

ingredients

250g quinoa

450ml cold water

250g salmon, strips (as fresh as
possible, best to get from fish
counter and ask for sashimi grade)

5 tbsp sushi seasoning vinegar

sea salt

7 sheets of nori seaweed

1 avocado, sliced lengthways into
14 strips

handful chives

3 tablespoon mayonnaise

toasted sesame seeds

garnish

soy sauce or teriyaki

pickled ginger

wasabi

Place the quinoa in a fine sieve, and under cold water until the water is clear (not cloudy), then leave to drain the through a strainer for around 30 minutes.

Add the quinoa to a saucepan with 450ml cold water. Bring to the boil, then cover and simmer on a low heat for 20 minutes.

Remove from the heat, carefully fluff with fork, then leave with the lid on to settle for 10 minutes.

Pour the quinoa onto a large platter, and coat all the grains with sushi seasoning vinegar. Then cool down the quinoa as soon as possible, you can use a fan or magazine!

The quinoa will become glossy as it absorbs the vinegar mixture, do not over stir as it will become mushy.

Cover with a damp cloth while making the sushi variations (Quinoa will keep up to 3 hours at room temperature. Do not refrigerate.).

Prepare your fillings: salmon, avocado and chives.

Cover a bamboo rolling mat in cling film, wrapping over a couple of times.

Fill a small bowl of water for sealing the edges of the nori sheets.

Place your rolling mat in front of you, cut off two sections from the top of the seaweed sheet (you will see an indentation) then place on to the rolling mat shiny-side facing down about 2cm from the edge.

Divide the quinoa into 7 heaps of, so you have enough for each roll.

Collect 1 heap of quinoa and place on the prepared seaweed sheet, spread the quinoa evenly, leaving 1cm margin at the top uncovered. Flatten the quinoa and make neat at the edges.

Place the mayonnaise 2cm from the closest part of the seaweed towards you along the width. Then place your fillings. Do not overload. You can also sprinkle some sesame seeds.

Lift the near edge of the rolling mat and fold it over the filling (holding the filling in place with your middle and forefingers,

LISA'S TIP

Cover a bamboo rolling mat in cling film, wrapping over a couple of times, to prevent your fillings getting caught in the mat. This way it keeps your mat nice and clean.

aiming to meet the top edge of the quinoa. Roll over approx. 3 times.

Lift the mat slightly to uncover the roll and remove your fingers from inside the roll, continue to roll until the two edges of the nori sheet meet.

Dip your fingertip in the water bowl and seal the top of the nori sheet.

Cover the roll with the rolling mat again and gently press along the length a couple of times, before removing the mat.

Place the rolls to the side until you have finished rolling, then using a serrated sharp knife, (and wiping the blade with a damp cloth to stop the quinoa from sticking) cut in the centre, then each half in two!

Asian Chicken Salad

This colourful, crunchy, tangy salad can be served at a picnic or
simply when you have leftover chicken or turkey!

{serves 4 - 6}

ingredients

1 whole cooked chicken, deboned and shredded

400g shredded red, white or Chinese cabbage

4 tsp sesame oil

1 tsp soya sauce

4 tbsp teriyaki sauce, gluten-free

6 tbsp sushi seasoning (sweet vinegar)

1 avocado, blended in a food processor until smooth

garnish

7g finely chopped chives (handful)

2 tbsp toasted sesame seeds

2 tbsp toasted cashew nuts

fresh coriander, roughly chopped

chilli flakes

Preparation time - 30 mins

Remove the skin from the pre-cooked chicken, debone and shred the white/dark meat. Place meat in a large bowl.

To the shredded chicken add the sesame oil, soya sauce and teriyaki sauce. Mix well then add the avocado.

Toast the sesame seeds in a dry frying pan on a gentle heat until golden. Remove the seeds from the heat and leave to cool.

In another large mixing bowl, add the shredded cabbage together with sushi seasoning (sweet vinegar).

Add your seasoned shredded chicken into the cabbage mixture and toss.

Using a pair of kitchen scissors, cut the chives over the salad bowl. Add the roughly chopped coriander.

Check for seasoning and add salt and pepper to taste.

Garnish with the toasted sesame seeds, toasted cashew nuts and chilli flakes.

LISA'S TIP

The heat of summer calls for grilling and quickly prepared salads. Once you have mastered this salad, you may like to vary it by adding some chili, shredded carrots, mango, or mint.

Moroccan Beef Parcels with Hummus

Gently spiced beef served over creamy hummus and crunchy lettuce.
Wonderful textures and exotic seasoning.

{serves 4 - 6}

ingredients

2 enchalion shallots, finely chopped

1/2 kilo lean mince beef

30g toasted pine nuts

2 tsp onion soup mix, gluten-free

sea salt, black pepper and white pepper

garlic granules

ground cinnamon

2 tsp acacia honey

2 tbsp coconut oil

1 handful fresh coriander

garnish

4 tbsp tahini

4 tbsp water

2/3 tsp lemon juice

handful coriander

250g hummus (make your own or shop bought)

4/6 baby gem lettuces, separated into leaves, to serve

chilli flakes

Preparation time - 40 mins, cooking time - 40 mins

In a non-stick frying pan, toast the pine nuts until lightly browned, then remove and place on a plate to cool.

Add 2 tbsp coconut oil, fry the shallots until translucent.

Now add the lean mince beef, and continue to stir, until the meat is browned for about 5 minutes over a medium heat.

Season generously with sea salt, black pepper, garlic granules, ground cinnamon and onion soup powder mix.

Continue back on the heat for a further 5 minutes, then add the honey and chopped fresh coriander.

Add the toasted pine nuts cook for a further 5 minutes on a low heat, then leave to cool.

Add the tahini, water, lemon juice, chopped coriander to a mini food chopper and blend together then season and check for consistency.

When you are ready to serve, place the beef mixture in a sharing bowl, place hummus in the base of the baby gem lettuces, then fill with the beef mixture and drizzle a little tahini over the top and sprinkle with chilli flakes.

LISA'S TIP

In the summer, dishes that combine warm meats and crunchy leaves are most welcome. This dish adds the creamy texture of hummus. Consider it a healthier version of a fully loaded burger (and tastier, too!).

Quinoa with Sautéed Leeks, Peas & Avocado

A summertime salad balancing soft
sautéed leeks and crunchy seeds.

....

{serves 4 - 6}

ingredients

300g quinoa
400ml cold water
3 leeks, sliced thinly
250g petit pois (frozen peas)
2 avocados, cubed
2 tbsp coconut or olive oil
60g pumpkin seeds
sea salt and white pepper
garlic granules

dressing

60ml olive oil
60ml apple juice
2 tsp honey mustard
2 tsp agave nectar
2 tbsp sushi seasoning vinegar
sesame seeds, toasted
1 handful fresh coriander, chopped
1 handful fresh mint leaves,
chopped

Preparation time - 40 mins, cooking time - 15 to 20 mins

Rinse the uncooked quinoa through a sieve with cold water, for 2 minutes, then drain well.

Place the quinoa in a medium saucepan with 400ml cold water, bring to boil, cover and simmer on a low heat for 15 minutes.

Remove from heat, carefully fluff with a fork, cover and stand for 5 minutes, then spread onto a large flat platter to cool.

In a large non-stick frying pan, add the oil, sauté the sliced leeks until translucent and soft, season with sea salt, white pepper and garlic granules.

Add the frozen peas to the sautéed leeks and continue to cook for 5 minutes, then remove from heat to cool.

Add sautéed leeks to the cooked quinoa, add the pumpkin seeds.

In a measuring jug, add the olive oil, apple juice, honey mustard, agave nectar, sushi seasoning vinegar, season with sea salt and black pepper.

Add the chopped mint, coriander and toasted sesame seeds.

When the salad is completely cooled, add the cubed chunks of avocado, mix through the salad then pour over the dressing.

LISA'S TIP

Picnic season is here. This quinoa salad is perfect for such an occasion, or really any summer night - it's light but satisfying, packed with plant based protein and packs well for dining al fresco.

Carrot & Courgette Soup

Carrot soup is naturally delicious and the addition of
leeks elevate it to a more sophisticated level.

{serves 4 - 6}

ingredients

1 1/3 kilo carrots, cubed
680g courgettes, sliced
2 large echalions shallots, sliced
1 celery stalk, cut in half
1 bay leaf
1 leek finely sliced
1 ¼ litre boiling water
2 tbsp olive oil
2 tbsp tomato purée
2 tbsp bouillon powder
1 tsp coconut sugar
sea salt and white pepper

garnish

chives, finely chopped
150g vegetable crisps
drizzle of olive oil

Preparation time - 30 mins, cooking time - 40 mins

In a large saucepan over medium heat sauté the shallots in olive oil until translucent approx. 5 minutes.

Add the sliced leeks, and sauté for 3 minutes with the onions.

Add the cubed carrots, continue to sauté for 3 minutes then add the courgettes.

Season with sea salt and white pepper.

Add the tomato paste and sugar, stir until the vegetables are coated.

Add your bouillon powder together with the boiling water. Add the celery stalks and bay leaf then bring back to a boil for 3-5 minutes.

Reduce the heat to medium and cook for 40 minutes (if you find there is a lot of broth on the top, using a large spoon you can skim that off).

Remove from the heat and cool slightly. Discard the celery stalk.

Using a hand held blender, purée the soup in the pot, or purée in batches in a blender or food processor.

If the soup is too thick, add a little extra boiling water (almond or soya milk are also good choices).

Garnish with vegetable crisps, a drizzle of olive oil and finely chopped chives.

LISA'S TIP

Did you know that if you eat a bowl of vegetable soup, you will feel full for a longer period of time than if you drink a glass of water and eat the vegetables separately. Your body and brain actually recognize water differently when it's combined with food. So get smart and eat soup often to help control your appetite. This soup also contains low-to-medium glycaemic index (GI) ingredients, is low in fat and contains a good source of dietary fibre.

Cucumber & Dill Salad

Cool and refreshingly different with
the addition of sushi seasoning.

{serves 4}

ingredients

2 large cucumbers, peeled, halved
and then sliced

2 tsp lemon juice

1 tsp sesame oil

4 tbsp sushi seasoning vinegar

2 tsp sweet chilli sauce

1 tsp agave nectar

1 bunch dill, chopped

1 bunch mint, chopped

1 handful chives, chopped

sea salt and white pepper

garnish

1 tbsp toasted sesame seeds

Preparation time - 30 mins

Peel each cucumber.

Cut the cucumbers in half down the length, scoop out the seeds with a teaspoon then cut slices down each length and place in a large mixing bowl.

Finely chop the mint, dill, chives and place in the bowl with the cucumbers and season with white pepper and a little sea salt.

In a separate small mixing bowl, add the lemon juice, sweet chilli, vinegar, sesame oil and agave nectar. Mix well then pour over the cucumbers.

Sprinkle with toasted sesame seeds.

LISA'S TIP

For me, cucumbers mean summer is almost here and I will be able to slice, dice, and chop fresh cucumbers into dishes of all shapes and forms. Clearly I love all things 'cucumbery' – who doesn't? This salad was inspired by those thinly sliced cucumbers marinated in rice vinegar that are sometimes served with sushi. This is a refreshing salad that is perfect for days when it's really scorching outside.

Pan Fried New Potatoes with Shallots

This dish is a true celebration of the season as Jersey Royals are only available for a short-time. Substitute new potatoes if you want a year-round dish!

{serves 4-6}

ingredients

750g new potatoes or Jersey Royals
5g rosemary sprigs
4 garlic cloves, crushed
4 echalion shallots cut in half
2-3 tbsp olive oil
sea salt and black pepper

Preparation time - 30 mins, cooking time - 40 mins

Wash potatoes to remove any excess dirt.

Bring a large pan of water to the boil, add potatoes, bring back to the boil, then simmer gently for 15-20 minutes or until soft. Drain then run under cold water.

Remove the skins of the shallots, cut in half and then, in a large non-stick frying pan, gently fry in the olive oil for 5 minutes and set aside.

Cut the potatoes in half lengthways then place the large non-stick frying pan with the shallots back on the stove for a further 5 minutes.

Add another tbsp olive oil, and season with sea salt, black pepper and crushed garlic.

Add the rosemary sprigs to the frying pan, continue shaking the pan over the heat, to ensure that you get the potatoes crispy.

Serve hot or cold.

LISA'S TIP

Do not peel Jersey potatoes. Simply rub any flaky skin gently from the surface. Always put into boiling salted water - to seal in the flavour. Jersey Royal potatoes are the crème de la crème of the potato world and they have a unique sweet buttery flavour and melt-in-the-mouth texture.

Gazpacho Soup

This cold soup comes from the southern part of Spain, Andalucia, where summer temperatures can reach over 100°F! If you choose to make a very smooth version of this soup, be sure to add a crunchy garnish for contrast.

....

{serves 4}

ingredients

10 large Jack Hawkins (or large beef) tomatoes, skins removed

2 ½ large cucumbers peeled and deseeded

1 small red onion

2 garlic clove

500ml V8 vegetable juice

4 tbsp sweet chilli sauce

4 tbsp white wine vinegar

2 tsp agave syrup

4 tbsp mayonnaise

salt & pepper

garnish

2 large cucumbers peeled, deseeded and finely chopped

4 medium tomatoes, deseeded and finely chopped

5 slices of wholemeal gluten-free bread

1 red onion finely chopped

To remove the skins from your tomatoes, make a criss-cross incision on the top and place in a pot of boiling water for 1 minute. Then immediately immerse in cold water to stop the cooking process. The skin will now come easily away.

Cut the skinned tomatoes into quarters, and place in a large mixing bowl.

Using a vegetable peeler, peel 2 ½ large cucumbers and deseed then cut into chunks and place in the mixing bowl with the tomatoes.

Cut the red onion into quarters and place in the mixing bowl.

Crush the garlic cloves.

Blend the tomatoes, cucumber, red onion and garlic together with the bottle of V8 juice in batches.

Pass the ingredients through a fine sieve and discard any pulp.

Then add sweet chilli sauce, white wine vinegar, mayonnaise and 2 tsp of agave nectar stir well.

Then add salt and pepper, then sieve again for a second time and stir well. Refrigerate for 45 minutes or overnight is best.

To make the croutons, remove crust from the bread then cut length ways into 4 strips, then cut each strip into 7 small equal pieces, cut each piece in half again.

Place the croutons on a non-stick baking tray with a good drizzle of olive oil and a sprinkle of sea salt.

Place in the oven on a baking tray on a medium heat for 10-12 minutes. Keep an eye on the croutons and shake the tray after the first 5 minutes.

When the croutons are a nice golden colour, remove from the oven, and leave to cool.

Garnish with finely chopped tomatoes, cucumber, red onion and croutons.

LISA'S TIP

This soup can be made the day before serving, making it ideal for dinner parties or lazy weekends. If serving adults, a small shot of vodka is a wonderful addition. Note: the soup will keep up to 3 days refrigerated.

Artichoke, Edamame Bean & Potato Salad

A deliciously different summertime salad
that can be served hot or cold.

{serves 4 - 6}

ingredients

400g artichoke bottoms, (frozen)

200g edamame beans, (frozen or fresh, cooked and peeled)

500g potatoes cut into 2cm cubes

6 tbsp olive oil

½ tsp lemon juice

large handful of dill, chopped

sea salt

white pepper

garnish

½ lemon sliced

Preparation time - 40 mins, cooking time - 20 mins

Bring a large pan of salted water to the boil. Add the frozen artichoke bottoms and cook for approx. 15-20 minutes covered, then drain.

Place the cubed potatoes in cold water. Bring to the boil and cook for 8 minutes, then drain under cold water.

Blanch the edamame beans in salted boiling water for 5 minutes. Drain, then place in a bowl filled with cold water and remove the bean husk.

Add 2 tbsp olive oil to a large non stick frying pan, add the cubed potatoes and cook for 5 minutes.

Add the edamame beans, season with sea salt and white pepper and cook for further 2-3 minutes.

Cut the artichoke bottoms in quarters or halves, depending on the size. Add to the frying pan, with the remaining 4 tbsp olive oil and cook for a further 5 minutes, add more seasoning if required.

Add the chopped dill, lemon juice and lemon slices.

Either serve warm or cold as a salad.

LISA'S TIP

This light and delicious summer salad combines zesty artichoke hearts with tender edamame beans. Artichokes! High in antioxidants and fibre, the flesh of these little beauties has a creamy flavour and texture despite their armoured exterior. I sometimes like to serve this salad with large shavings of parmesan cheese. Alternatively, this complements my Lamb Chops with Coriander & Mint.

Chicken & Cashews with Broccoli

A lighter, healthier version of
the Chinese takeaway treat.

{serves 4}

ingredients

2 tbsp peanut oil

1 tsp sesame oil

500g chicken breast fillets, sliced thinly

1 clove garlic, crushed

1 small leek, sliced thinly

1 red onion, sliced thinly

1 medium carrot, sliced thinly

250g broccoli, chopped coarsely

1 tsp cornflour

125ml chicken stock

2 tbsp teriyaki sauce

garnish

75g unsalted roasted cashews

fresh coriander

toasted sesame seeds

250g black gluten-free noodles

Preparation time - 30 mins, cooking time - 30 mins

Season the thinly sliced chicken pieces with salt & pepper.

Heat half of the peanut oil, with the sesame oil in a wok or a large frying pan. Stir fry the chicken in batches, depending on the size of your pan, until browned, for around 2-3 minutes, with a splash of teriyaki sauce. Now set aside.

Heat the remaining peanut oil in the wok, stir fry the red onion, garlic, leek, carrot and broccoli until leek is soft. Add the carrot and broccoli and cook for 5 minutes.

Pour boiling water into your measuring jug with half a chicken stock cube, then mix in your corn flour.

Return the chicken to the wok with the chicken stock and teriyaki sauce. Stir and check for taste, seasoning if necessary.

Stir fry for about 8 minutes, then sprinkle with the roasted cashew nuts, toasted sesame seeds and fresh coriander.

Serve with your choice of brown rice or gluten-free noodles.

LISA'S TIP

Check that you have all the ingredients you need ahead of time. Make sure all the food is cut according to directions before you start. Never try to prepare food while stir-frying and be sure to cut all the ingredients the same size. Pre-heat the wok on medium-high to high heat for at least a minute before adding oil.

Thai Seared Beef & Mushroom Salad

Good quality meat is a must for
this quickly prepared dish.

{serves 4 - 6}

ingredients

500g fillet steak or rib eye, cut into portions, or as a loin

2 tbsp coconut oil

150g oyster mushrooms, sliced

150g shiitake mushrooms, stems removed and sliced

1 tbsp honey

1 tbsp soy sauce light

dressing

3 spring onions, finely chopped

2 garlic gloves, finely minced

1 lime, juice

2 tbsp fresh coriander

2 tbsp fish sauce

3 tsp palm sugar

2 tbsp honey

1 tbsp sweet chilli sauce

garnish

1 romaine lettuce

1 whole cucumber, deseeded and cut into thin strips

175g cherry tomatoes

2 tbsp sesame seeds

Big bunch of coriander

1 handful roughly chopped roasted peanuts

Preparation time - 30 mins, cooking time 8 to 15 mins

Place a large non-stick frying pan on the stove, place the steak in the pan and seal each side for 2-4 minutes or until done to your liking. In total cooking times are as follows: (6-8 minutes for rare; 7-10 for medium-rare; 10-12 minutes for medium/well-done). Once cooked, leave to rest for 15 minutes (please note that the meat will continue to cook when removed from the heat).

Make the dressing by mixing all the ingredients in a bowl, leave to stand and infuse.

Clean the mushrooms, remove the stalks from the shiitakes, then slice.

Heat the coconut oil in a frying pan, add the sliced shiitake and oyster mushrooms, cook for 5-10 minutes until the juices have evaporated, then add the soy sauce and honey and cook for a further 3 minutes.

Remove the frying pan from the heat and leave the mushrooms to cool.

Slice the meat as thinly as possible, or to your liking, then add the meat to the mushrooms in the pan to soak up the juices. (If you are unsure about the rareness of your meat, you can cook the meat for a couple of minutes on each side with the mushrooms), or just baste all the ingredients together and leave in the pan, off the heat.

Wash and finely shred the lettuce, cut the tomatoes in half, and place in a large serving bowl or platter with the cucumber strips.

Place the mushrooms and steak in a separate bowl, then pour over the dressing, stir the mixture a couple of times to ensure that the meat is coated.

Spoon the steak mixture in the centre of your serving dish and sprinkle the sesame seeds, roughly chopped peanuts and top with coriander.

LISA'S TIP

Exceptionally moreish, you may wish to add a spoon of brown rice or two to help soak up all the wonderful juices!

Thai Chicken Curry

A creamy, citrusy dish full of the
flavours of Southeast Asia.

{serves 4 - 6}

ingredients

2 sweet potatoes cut into 5cm strips
and then halved

4 tbsp garden peas

400g broccoli florets

1 aubergine chopped into small
cubes

100g baby corn, cut in half
lengthways

1 tbsp vegetable or sunflower oil

1 garlic clove, chopped

1-2 tbsp Thai green curry paste
(plus a little extra if you like it
spicy)

1 tbsp Thai fish sauce (Nam pla)

4 tsp palm sugar

4 chicken breast (breasts or thighs),
cut into bite-size pieces

3 wide strips lime zest, plus extra to
garnish or basil leaves

1 tsp Madras curry (optional)

2 x 400ml coconut milk

2 tbsp coconut yogurt

garnish

Thai basil leaves or fresh coriander
wholegrain rice, to serve

Preparation time - 30 mins - Cooking time 20 to 30 mins

Put the sweet potatoes in a pan of boiling water and cook for 5 minutes, then remove with a slotted spoon and throw in the broccoli florets and cook for a further 3 minutes. Remove the broccoli, add the baby corn and cook for 3 minutes, by which time all should be just tender. Put to one side.

In a wok or large frying pan, gently heat the oil, add garlic and cook until golden, this should take only a few seconds. Don't let it overcook.

Spoon in the curry paste and stir it around for a few seconds to begin to cook the spices and release all the flavours.

Next, pour in half of one tin of coconut milk and let it start to bubble. Now add the rest of the tin. Only use one tin at this point.

Stir in the fish sauce and palm sugar. Then add the pieces of chicken and aubergine, cook on a medium to high heat, then turn the heat down to a simmer and cook, covered, for about 15-20 minutes until the chicken is cooked through and the sauce is slightly reduced and thickened.

Tip in the sweet potatoes, broccoli florets, baby corn and garden peas and let them warm through in sauce, if the coconut milk has reduced too much, add the second tin slowly to 'top up' depending on the amount that you need and cook for a further 10 minutes.

Check for taste as you may wish to add more Thai curry paste at this point.

Then add a lovely 'citrusy' flavour by stirring in the shredded lime leaves (or lime zest). The basil leaves go in next, but only leave them briefly on the heat or they will quickly lose their brightness. Check for seasoning, adding more fish sauce if needed.

Add in 2 tbsp of coconut yogurt and Madras curry powder (optional).

The curry is now best left to sit for a few minutes so the sauce becomes creamier.

Serve with wholegrain rice.

LISA'S TIP

If you have left over roast chicken you can also add towards the end (instead of cooking from raw) to heat through. This recipe will keep for a few days in the refrigerator.

Whole Baked Sea Bass in Banana Leaves

The banana leaves make for a bit of 'high drama' at the dinner table. You can also use foil but double it to ensure there are no holes for steam to escape.

{serves 4 - 6}

ingredients

1 whole sea bass, 1.5kg, scaled, gutted, and fins removed

1 tbsp lime juice mixed with 1 tsp of salt and 2 tsp of palm sugar

paste

1 small onion roughly chopped

1 inch fresh root ginger, peeled and roughly chopped

1 Thai red chilli, deseeded and roughly chopped

2 garlic cloves

1 lemon grass stalk

125ml coconut milk

½ tsp chilli flakes

15g fresh coriander

1-2 tbsp honey

2 large pinches sea salt

banana leaves or foil for wrapping (if using banana leaves, make sure you clean them with warm water and kitchen paper first)

1 tbsp peanut oil

1 tsp sesame oil

garnish

coriander

lime wedges

preparation time - 30 mins, cooking time - 30-35 mins

Preheat the oven to 400°F, gas mark 6, 200°C (180°C fan-assisted)

Wash the sea bass inside and out, pat dry with kitchen paper.

If you are using banana leaves, wash carefully under cold water, and wipe clean with paper towels.

Score through the skin of the fish 3-4 times on each side, and rub the slits with the lime juice mixed with the palm sugar on both sides.

Then lay the fish on a large piece of oiled foil or banana leaves using peanut and sesame oil.

Put the lemongrass, chilli, chilli flakes, onion, garlic gloves, coriander, ginger and sea salt into a pestle & mortar or food processor and purée until smooth. Towards the end of grinding or puréeing slowly add 1 -2 tbsp of honey and the coconut milk.

Season the fish inside and out with the paste, and making sure you push some into the scored slits.

To wrap the fish in the banana leaves, begin by folding the sides of the leaf inward, then fold the top and bottom over and tucking the ends under (kind of like making a banana leaf burrito!). Using foil, wrap 2 layers securely around the fish, making sure there are no holes in the parcel. Tie with dampened string if you are using banana leaves.

Place in the pre-heated oven and cook for 30-35 minutes, until flesh is tender. If you're eating the fish straight away, let it rest for about 5 minutes before opening the parcel.

When ready to serve, garnish with lime wedges and coriander.

LISA'S TIP

You'll love this tender and wonderful-tasting Thai baked fish. Wrapping the sea bass in a banana leaf ensures the fish remains moist and imparts a subtle flavour. Banana leaves can be found in Thai and certain Asian grocers. However, foil can be used as a substitute. I like to serve with some brown rice to soak up the juices and wok fried pak choi. If you have extra paste, combine it with any leftover coconut milk, heat through in a small saucepan and strain through a fine sieve to serve drizzled over the fish as a delicious thai spice infused sauce.

Oven Baked Corn Flake Chicken Breast with Salsa

Gluten-free corn flakes make a wonderful substitute for breadcrumbs, and since it is oven-baked rather than fried, you save on calories, too.

{serves 4}

ingredients

4 chicken breast
150-200g gluten-free corn flakes
2 tbsp toasted sesame seeds
1 egg
2 tsp honey Dijon mustard
2 tsp Worcestershire sauce
garlic granules
sea salt and white pepper
cooking oil spray

avocado salsa

1 mango
3 avocados
2 tbsp olive oil
¼ red onion, finely chopped
2 tsp sweet chilli sauce

garnish

2 limes, cut into wedges
4 handfuls rocket

Preparation time - 40 mins, cooking time - 40 mins

Preheat the oven to 400°F, gas mark 6, 200°C (180°C fan-assisted).

Spray the cooking oil onto your baking tray.

Wash your chicken breast and dry with paper towels.

Place the corn flakes in a plastic bag and crush with your hands until the flakes have broken down. On a plate, combine with a sprinkle of sesame seeds, sea salt and white pepper. Toss together.

In a separate bowl large enough to hold the two chicken breast at a time, crack the whole egg and beat.

Season the egg with the Worcestershire sauce, honey Dijon mustard, garlic granules, and a bit more sea salt and white pepper.

Coat the chicken breast in the egg mixture then carefully place the chicken breast on the plate with the seasoned corn flakes, and coat both sides, repeat with the remaining breast, place on the baking tray.

Cook in the preheated oven for 40 minutes, ensuring presentation side (rounded part of the breast) is facing up.

To make the avocado salsa, halve the avocados, remove the stone and peel away the skin, cut the flesh into 1cm cubes and place in a large bowl.

Peel the mango and cut both sides close to the pip, then into 1cm cubes, then add to the same bowl as the avocado, mix together with the finely chopped red onion.

Add the olive oil, sweet chili and season with sea salt and black pepper.

Gently stir the ingredients; you can mash the avocado slightly, but keep it quite chunky.

Remove the chicken breast from the oven and rest for 8 minutes before cutting.

Garnish with the avocado salsa with rocket and wedge or two of lime.

LISA'S TIP

The mango has an oblong pit in the centre. Cut along the sides of the pit, separating the flesh from the pit then, taking a mango half, use a knife to make lengthwise and crosswise cuts in it, but try not to cut through the peel. At this point you may be able to pull the segments right off of the peel with your fingers.

Frozen Berries Coconut Sorbet

A delicious dairy free treat that doesn't require an ice cream maker. You can eat this as soon as it's made if you like a soft scoop – or freeze overnight for a firmer texture.

{serves 4}

ingredients

2 bananas ripe, frozen (3cm slices)

125g blackberries, frozen

300g strawberries, stems removed, frozen

200g blueberries, frozen

100g coconut milk yogurt (coyo)

2 tsp date syrup

2 handfuls of granola, (gluten-free)

Preparation time - 20 mins, freezing fruit 6 to 8 hours (overnight - is best) freezing sorbet 6 to 8 hours (overnight- is best)

Remove the frozen fruits from the freezer, 20 minutes before blending.

Place all the frozen fruits in the bowl of your food processor and process for 1 minute at a time, stirring with a spatula as required. Repeat 3-4 times until well blended.

Add the coconut yogurt together with the date syrup, and blend for another 30 seconds.

Transfer to a freezer safe container and freeze until required or serve immediately.

When serving, sprinkle some granola over the top.

LISA'S TIP

A good first dessert to make with children. A sneaky way to get in your five-a-day!

Seasonal Fruit Tart with Crème Patisserie

Admittedly, this recipe takes time but be patient. The result is a stunning dessert which resembles a painter's palette of brilliant colours.

....

{serves 10-12}

date & walnut pastry

300g pitted dates
250g ground walnuts
150g ground almonds
pinch salt

crème patisserie

600ml almond milk
1 vanilla pod
6 egg yolks (large)
100g coconut sugar
50g oat flour, wheat & gluten-free
10g corn flour

seasonal fruit

500g strawberries, hulled and thinly sliced
150g blueberries
1 tbsp apricot jam (sugar free, smooth variety), 1 tsp cold water

Preparation time - 2 hours - Cooling - 30 - 40 mins

To make the pastry you will need a food processor.

Place the dates in the food processor, and blend till smooth then add the ground walnuts and almonds, a pinch of salt and process till smooth.

When the pastry forms a ball, stop the machine.

Line the base of a 23cm fluted, loose bottom non-stick tart tin with parchment paper. Then, by hand push, the mixture into the base and against the sides to form the pastry for the tart. ensuring it is level all the way around and on the base.

Place another piece of parchment paper over the pasty and place in the freezer for 20 minutes. Remove and place in the fridge.

To make the crème patisserie, cut the vanilla pod in half lengthways. Remove the seeds with the back of a knife running down the length of the pod. Place the seeds and pod into the almond milk in a saucepan on a gentle heat for 5 minutes for the vanilla to infuse the milk (be careful that the milk does not burn).

Place the egg yolks and sugar together in a bowl and beat until white and smooth. Now slowly whisk in the oat flour and corn flour until you have a smooth paste.

Remove the milk from the stove, then slowly whisk the milk into the egg mixture using a balloon whisk. Mix slowly and carefully until all the ingredients are thoroughly blended.

Pour the liquid through a sieve directly into the saucepan, pushing through the vanilla seeds. Discard the pod.

Place back on the stove and bring the vanilla cream to the boil, whisking it continuously. Continue to cook for 2-3 minutes to get rid of the starchy taste of the corn flour. It is important to continue whisking or mixture will stick.

LISA'S TIP

To decorate the tart its best to use fresh fruits (such as berries, bananas, oranges, kiwifruit, plums, pineapple, and melon). Prepare the fruit by gently washing and drying. Peel and slice the bananas, plums and kiwifruit. The strawberries will need to be sliced also. Arranging the fruit on the tart can be done either randomly or in concentric overlapping circles, starting at the outside edge. Try to cover the filling completely so none of the cream mixture shows.

If you feel that you haven't reached the correct consistency after 3 minutes, reduce the heat to medium/low and continue whisking. You should start to feel the crème thickening and you will notice your hand aching by now, but don't give up! You are looking for a thick consistency (once again be careful not to burn the cream).

Pour the vanilla cream into a bowl or baking tray to cool, cover with cling film and place in the fridge for 30-40 minutes until chilled.

Remove the pastry from the fridge.

Prepare all your fruits by washing and slicing, so that everything is ready to hand.

Remove the crème patisserie from the fridge, beat the mixture together until smooth, if necessary, the thick cold cream can be strained through a fine sieve and stirred until smooth, then place the mixture into a piping bag.

Pipe out the crème patisserie starting in the middle and follow around in a circle motion until you get to the edge then smooth out with the back of a spoon

Assemble your mixed fruit strawberries and blueberries.

For the apricot glaze: heat the apricot jam in a small saucepan over a medium heat until it has melted. You can add a touch of water if the consistency is too thick, let cool until it is only slightly warm, then using a pastry brush glaze the tart.

Banana Ice Cream with Halva

This is my favourite magic trick in the kitchen: creamy ice cream made with just bananas! The other ingredients are added just for fun. Now gather around and watch!

....

{serves 4 - 6}

ingredients

6 frozen, ripe bananas, cut into 3cm slices

100g vanilla halva, chopped

40g dark chocolate, melted

40g banana chips, ground

Preparation time - 20 mins, freezing time - 4 to 6 hours (or overnight is best)

Peel the bananas and cut into 3cm slices and place in a freezer bag or zip lock containers and freeze until solid - around 4 to 6 hours, or overnight is best.

Place the banana chips in a food processor and process until fully ground.

Melt the dark chocolate and leave to cool slightly.

Remove the bananas 5-10 minutes before processing to help thaw out.

Place the bananas in the food processor and blend away, you will have to keep scraping down the sides every so often.

Watch as the magic happens when bananas turn into ice-cream! It should take approx. 3 minutes. At first you will think 'how is this ever going to be soft and creamy'? The answer is *patience* and wait for the surprise!

Within a few minutes, you'll be able to process the mixture into a thick and creamy, ice-cream-like dessert.

Scoop out into a large bowl and fold in the chopped halva.

Serve with melted chocolate and sprinkled with ground banana chips.

Then serve straight away to your guests if you like it semi-soft. Or you can freeze for a few hours to make it scoop-able.

LISA'S TIP

Freeze ripe bananas until solid, then whiz them up in a blender or food processor, it gets creamy and a little gooey, just like ice cream. And what's more exciting, it has no additional dairy, wheat, gluten, sweeteners, additives or preservative! For toppings try: crushed almonds and honey, cocoa powder and cashew butter, granola, or even some more sliced bananas.

Raw Blueberry Cheesecake

Made with a vegan crust, this cheesecake is surprisingly delicious –
bursting with antioxidants from the blueberries.

{serves 12 - 14}

crust Ingredients

100g macadamia nuts

150g blanched almonds

50g desiccated coconut

200g dates, (pre-soak if hard)

3 tsp lemon juice

1 pinch sea salt

cheesecake layer ingredients

250g cashews, soaked overnight in
water, then rinsed and drained on
paper towel until ready to use

60ml coconut oil

60ml agave nectar, maple syrup or
honey

2 tsp custard powder

5 tsp lemon juice

100g blueberries (splitting the
mixture)

blueberry chia seed topping

240g blueberries

4 tsp agave nectar

6 tsp chia seeds

2 tsp lemon juice

Preparation time - 60 mins, soaking time - 8 hours (or overnight is best)

First, pre-soak the cashews, covered with cold water overnight for 8 hours.

Line the base and sides of 20cm non-stick springform tin with parchment paper.

To make the chia seed topping, place the blueberries in the food processor and blend until smooth. Sieve over a bowl to omit the skins and seeds. Add agave nectar, lemon juice, and chia seeds. Mix together then refrigerate for 2 hours.

For the crust, place the macadamia, blanched almond and coconut into your food processor and pulse until a chunky sandy consistency. Place into a clean bowl.

Add the dates, lemon and salt to the food processor, blend until smooth and then add the macadamia nut mixture back into the food processor, and blend until it forms a ball.

Place the nut and date mixture into your prepared tin, press down firmly and place in the freezer.

Place all cheesecake filling ingredients (expect blueberries) into your food processor and blend for 5 minutes until completely smooth (stopping to scrape down the sides).

Remove the crust after 10 minutes from the freezer.

Pour about 1/2 of the filling mixture onto the crust and smooth with a spatula, then place back in the freezer.

Add the blueberries to the remaining filling and blend on high until smooth, then pour onto the first layer of filling. Place in freezer until solid - about 2 hours.

Then add the chia seed topping. The seeds will have started to congeal together so loosen them slightly, then smooth over the cheesecake and decorate with blueberries and place back in the fridge to set for 1 hour.

Release the cake from the tin when ready to serve.

LISA'S TIP

Cheesecakes are always a good place to start when making raw desserts because the process is so quick and simple. And what's more exciting is that it's wheat, gluten and dairy free.

AUTUMN

seasonal moods

Without warning, the days gain a crisp, energising feel and the trees put on their autumn coats. Burnt oranges, vibrant reds and golden brown is the palette of Autumn both in the landscape and on our plates.

Apples, pumpkins, and sweet potatoes are in abundance and, combined with a touch of ginger, turn magical. The smell of roasting chestnuts or the simply oven-seared figs add to the fragrance of Autumn.

It is the time of year when we take stock and review where we've been. Is it a path to continue or to change?

APPLES Crisp English apples perfectly sum up the arrival of autumn. Containing bone strengthening boron and cholesterol lowering pectin, the old expression might be right! Try apple cider vinegar on salads for additional benefits.

FIGS Look for slightly soft and ripe figs when shopping as they don't ripen once picked. Naturally sweet, figs are ideal for healthier baking. Also, its potassium content is high which serves to negate the effects of sodium on the body.

CHESTNUTS The warm, nutty smell of roasting chestnuts is one of the joys of this season. They are also low in fat, high in fibre and chock full of minerals. Eat them to help boost your immune system.

GINGER Ginger has been prescribed for hundreds of years to relieve digestive problems, but new research shows that this root's real power is in reducing inflammation. Look for a thin skinned variety when shopping as this indicates the ginger is young.

BUTTERNUT SQUASH Offers a great source of vitamins B1, B6 and C. Perfect now as vitamin C boosts your immune system. Like beets, try butternut squash roasted for exceptional flavour!

PEARS Often described as hypoallergenic (allergies to them are rare), pears are often the first fruit we taste. They are considered the perfect weaning food for babies who are attempting solids. As adults, we love them poached in red wine or served with melted dark chocolate.

AUBERGINES Whether you called them 'aubergine', 'eggplant' or 'brinjal', this vegetable – which is actually a berry – can be found all over the world in local cuisine. Originally grown in India, they can now be found in many shapes, sizes and colours around the globe.

PECANS The buttery and almost maple syrup-like tang of pecan nuts is unmistakable. Part of the hickory family, pecans originate from the Americas and are among the top 15 most anti-oxidant-rich foods.

Dried Fig, Pecan & Dark Chocolate Oat Bars

Slightly decadent, but less so than store bought brands, these
bars are good for breakfast or as a lunch box treat.

....

{makes 16 bars}

ingredients

150ml coconut oil

120g agave nectar

2 tbsp date syrup

225g rolled oats, wheat & gluten-
free

20g sunflower seeds

60g pecans, chopped in half

100g dried figs, sliced into strips

35g dark chocolate raisins

20g desiccated coconut

sea salt, 2 pinches

cinnamon

**Preparation time - 30 mins, cooking time - 35-40 mins, refrigeration
time - 1 hour to firm**

Preheat the oven to 300°F gas mark 2, 150°C (130°C fan-assisted).

Line a 23cm x 23cm baking tray with parchment paper.

Over a gentle heat melt the coconut oil, agave and date syrup until
smooth set aside.

In a large mixing bowl add the rolled oats, salt, cinnamon, chopped
pecans, sliced dried figs, desiccated coconut, sunflower seeds and
dark chocolate raisins. Mix well.

Pour over the oil mixture, mix well and then place in the prepared
baking tray. Press down firmly until smooth.

Bake in the preheated oven for 35-40 minutes or until golden.

Let cool in the baking tray, then place in the fridge to harden up.

When ready to serve, lift out of the tin and cut into squares. Place
back in the fridge if you have spare.

Yum.

LISA'S TIP

*These oat bars can be stored in an airtight container for up to one
week in the refrigerator. These are perfect for breakfast on the run as
they are filled with protein and fibre. Once you start to perfect these
bars, you can play around with the nut and fruit ingredients.*

Shakshuka

This is my version and it has a twist! I'm not a fan of peppers, so I add shiitake mushrooms and kale. If you want more heat, add some chilli flakes or a touch of Tabasco.

··

{serves 4 -6}

ingredients

6 large eggs

500ml pasta tomato sauce (jarred)

50g curly kale, stems removed

1 large onion, sliced thinly

125g shiitake mushrooms, thinly sliced, stems removed

4 tbsp coconut oil

sea salt and white pepper

garlic granules

garnish

cracked black pepper

Preparation time - 30 mins, cooking time - 31 to 33 mins

Heat the coconut oil in a large frying pan, and sauté the thinly sliced onions for 5 minutes until soft and translucent.

Add the sliced shiitake mushrooms, cook for 2 minutes and at this point you should notice the mushrooms soaking up the oil. Season well with sea salt, white pepper and garlic granules and cook for further 3 minutes.

Add the curly kale and cook for 5 minutes, continuously stirring.

Pour in the tomato sauce and cook for 10 minutes on a low heat to reduce the sauce.

Remove from the heat, crack the egg into a wine glass, then make a little well in the sauce and pour in the whole egg, repeat with each egg.

Place the frying pan back on the heat and cook covered for 6-8 minutes until the egg is set.

Then serve straight from the pan with a sprinkle of black pepper.

LISA'S TIP

'What the heck is Shakshuka?' you might be asking. It's a delicious tomatoey (sometimes spicy) Middle Eastern egg dish that's become very popular. I love to serve this dish with fresh avocado on the side and some gluten-free bread to wipe up the delicious sauce!

Bircher Autumnal Muesli

Usually enjoyed at breakfast, this dish also
makes a scrumptious dessert!

{serves 4 - 6}

ingredients

200g jumbo rolled oats, gluten-free
10g pistachios whole
10g almonds whole
10g pecans, whole
20g sultanas
4 dried figs, cut into small strips
(remove stalk)
1 pink lady apple, cored and grated
(keep skin on)
2 tbsp agave syrup
600ml almond milk
2 tbsp coconut yogurt (coyo)
cinnamon, sprinkle

garnish

2 figs quartered
honey
2 pinches coconut sugar
desiccated coconut, handful

Preparation time - 20 mins, refrigeration 8 hours (overnight)

In a large mixing bowl, add the rolled oats, cinnamon, grated apple, pistachios, almonds, pecans, sultanas and dried figs. Mix well.

In a measuring jug, add the almond milk, agave nectar, and coconut yogurt. Beat together with a mini hand whisk or fork, then pour over the oats.

Gently stir everything together, then cover and place in fridge for 8 hours.

Preheat the oven to 350°F, gas mark 4, 180°C (160°C fan-assisted).

Line a small baking tray with parchment paper, place the quartered figs on the tray, drizzle with honey and 2 pinches of coconut sugar.

Bake in the preheated oven for 10 minutes, then leave to cool.

When ready to serve, place the bircher muesli in serving bowls, place the quartered figs, drizzle a little juice from the figs and sprinkle with desiccated coconut.

LISA'S TIP

I love to have a big batch of bircher muesli in the fridge, it's the perfect breakfast when you're in a hurry. You can keep this in the fridge for 2-3 days. Be adventurous with your fillings, once you get the hang of making it. For cooler mornings heat the Bircher muesli on the stove for 2-3 minutes.

Sweet Potato Latke with Poached Eggs

While this is a complete dish, consider using the latkes alone to be served with a hearty beef stew. For something a bit special, add quail's eggs instead.

{makes 10 Latkes}

ingredients

675g Maris Piper potatoes (approx. 3 large) grated

250g sweet potato, grated

1 white onion, grated

60g fine cornmeal flour sifted

½ tsp baking powder, (gluten-free)

1 large egg

1 large egg yolk

sea salt and white pepper

500ml sunflower oil

garnish

4 tbsp crème fraiche

225g smoked salmon

4 large eggs

2 tsp vinegar

small handful chives, chopped

sprig of dill

Preparation time - 60 mins, cooking time - 20 mins

Grate the potatoes using the coarse side of the grater or a food processor. Place in a clean tea towel and squeeze out as much liquid as you can, then place the potato in a bowl (you want your moisture from other ingredients, not the potato).

Grate the sweet potato and onion and place in the same bowl as the white potato. In a separate bowl, beat the whole egg, and egg yolk. Season generously with sea salt and white pepper and mix well with potato mixture.

Add the sifted fine cornmeal flour and mix well. Using a 2.5cm round cutter, place a large tablespoon of filling into the cutter, with a chopping board underneath, squeeze the filling until level, lift off the cutter and repeat with the remaining mixture.

Place a large frying pan on the stove, add the oil on a medium/high heat. Using a spatula carefully slide off the latkes into the hot oil, fry over moderate heat until brown on the underside (approx. 3-4 minutes), then flip over using a fork and spatula (approx. 3-4 minutes) until crisp and golden.

Remove from the pan, drain on paper towel and serve hot. Keep a lined tray ready for the latkes to keep warm in the oven as you make more batches… They'll also cook through a little more in the oven. Don't stack! You can't leave the latkes in the frying pan too long because the natural sugar content of the sweet potato it will blacken easily - which is why it's important you don't have your stovetop heat on too high.

Poach the eggs to your liking in simmering water with a little vinegar for 3-4 minutes, then dry on paper towels.

Stack two potato pancakes per person with the egg on top. Add a spoonful of crème fraiche, with a sprig of dill and a smoked salmon flower (roll the smoked salmon and crunch together by the sides), and sprinkle with the chives.

LISA'S TIP

Always use fresh eggs when poaching and add a little vinegar to the water. This holds the egg's protein together. Another trick is to break the eggs into a cup first, then add to the simmering water.

Cauliflower Pizza Base with Blue Cheese, Pear & Walnuts

I can sense you are scratching your head at this one
– trust me, it works and is absolutely delicious!

....

{makes an 8 - 10 inch pizza}

ingredients

1 medium cauliflower head

70g grated mozzarella cheese (50g for the crust/20g for the topping)

1 egg, beaten

garlic granules

topping

1 pear, thinly sliced

20g walnuts

50g blue cheese, crumbled

olive oil, mild

garnish

rocket leaves

sea salt and pepper to taste

Preparation time - 60 mins, cooking time - 28 to 30 mins

Preheat the oven to 400°F, gas mark 6, 200°C (180°C fan-assisted) and pre-line a baking tray with parchment paper.

Wash and thoroughly dry the cauliflower. Cut off the florets, you don't need much stem, just stick with the florets. Pulse in your food processor for about 30 seconds, until you get powdery snow-like cauliflower. Place the cauliflower in a microwave safe bowl and cover, microwave for 4 minutes or steam. When cooked, place onto a clean tea towel and allow to cool.

Now wrap up the cauliflower in the tea towel and wring out all the liquid. Don't be alarmed with what you have left! Place the cauliflower into a bowl. Add 50g of the grated mozzarella cheese. Beat the egg, season generously with sea salt, white pepper and garlic granules. Pour onto the cauliflower mixture and combine well. Now use your hands to form the 'dough' into a crust on your parchment paper (aim for about 8-10 inches/20cm-25cm). Pat it down thoroughly, you want it nice and tightly formed together, don't make it too thick or thin either.

Bake for 20 minutes, until it starts to turn golden brown. Remove from oven. Leave the base to cool for 5-10 minutes, then carefully turn the base over and place back on the tray. Drizzle a little olive oil and sea salt on the cauliflower base, then top with thinly sliced pear, scatter the blue cheese and walnuts.

Season with a little black pepper and olive oil. Top with remaining grated mozzarella cheese and bake in the oven for 8-10 minutes. Garnish with rocket and serve.

LISA'S TIP

This is the best invention ever! Especially if you are following a gluten-free diet. Add whatever toppings you like! Who would have thought you could make a pizza base out of a vegetable! It's so delicious, that you won't think twice about wishing you made it with flour and yeast! And yes you can pick it up just like a real pizza!

Aromatic Crispy Duck Salad

One of the most popular dishes I make,
I often make two ducks at a time!

....

{serves 4 - 6}

ingredients

1 whole duck, roughly 2kg in weight

Chinese 5 spice powder

pinch of sea salt

1 onion

7 tbsp hoisin sauce, plus a bit extra

garnish

1 ½ tbsp sesame oil

1 large cucumber, deseeded (julienned or spiralised)

crispy salad onions (gluten-free)

sesame seeds, toasted (amount to taste)

2 handfuls cashew nuts, toasted

Preparation time - 40 mins, cooking time - 1 hour 52 mins

Preheat the oven to 400°F, gas mark 6, 200°C (180°C fan-assisted).

Wash and thoroughly dry the duck with paper towel. Drying it makes the skin crispy. Using a wooden skewer, prick the upper part of the breast and in-between the breast and thigh. Cut the onion into quarters, keeping the root intact. Rub 1 tbsp. sesame oil over both sides of the duck. Season with salt and Chinese 5 spice inside and out of the cavity.

Place duck on a wire rack over a large foil-lined baking tray. Bake in the preheated oven for 1 hour, breast facing down. Remove from the oven and carefully turn, breast facing up. Bake for 20 minutes then turn over, breast down. Reduce temperature to 300°F, gas mark 2, 150°C (130°C fan-assisted) for 20 minutes. Remove, leaving the duck to rest for 10 minutes.

Take off all the skin and place it on a clean, foil-lined tray. To the skin, rub in 1 tbsp hoisin sauce then increase the oven temperature back to 400°F, gas mark 6, 200°C (180°C fan-assisted) and bake for 10-12 minutes until crispy. Remove the duck bones and shred the meat into a large mixing bowl. When slightly cooled, add 3 tbsp hoisin sauce and massage into the meat. Let cool completely. Deseed the cucumber then julienne or spiralise it.

On a large serving platter place the cucumber, drizzle with 2 tsp of the sesame oil, then sprinkle with toasted sesame seeds. Add the shredded duck and top with shredded crispy skin. To garnish, drizzle 2-3 tbsp hoisin sauce and sprinkle a few toasted sesame seeds, crispy salad onions and toasted cashew nuts on top.

LISA'S TIP

Both children and adults go mad for this salad! Serve with duck pancakes on the side should you wish! I like to use baby gem lettuce instead.

Fresh Fig & Goats Cheese Salad

A simple and yet delectable salad of grilled fruit and nuts all served with a walnut oil and honey fig dressing. Makes for an elegant lunch or a refreshing starter.

{serves 4 - 6}

ingredients

8 fresh figs, (4 cut in half and 4 make a cut like a cross in the top of each fig)

150g goats cheese, crumbled

2 tsp acacia honey

2 handfuls toasted walnuts, crumbled

1 handful pistachios, roughly chopped

2 handfuls pomegranate seeds

1 large handful rocket

2 tbsp walnut oil

sea salt and black pepper

Preparation time - 30 mins, cooking time - 10 mins

Preheat the grill to a high setting, line a baking tray with foil or parchment paper.

Wash and stem the figs.

Slice 4 figs in half and arrange cut side up in a baking dish together. With the remaining 4 figs, cut a cross in the top of the figs to about half way down the fig so that they open up a bit if gently squeezed at the bottom.

Drizzle the honey over top of the figs.

Roast for about 10 minutes, or until the honey is just beginning to bubble.

The figs should not be too soft, be careful not to burn them - you need to be able to pick them up with your fingers.

Let cool for about 10 minutes before assembling the salad (keep the juice from the tray).

Place the figs on the serving platter. Scatter over the crumbled goats cheese, crumbled walnuts, roughly chopped pistachios and pomegranate seeds.

Drizzle with walnut olive oil and 1 tbsp of fig juice from the baking tray.

Sprinkle a little sea salt and black pepper then garnish with rocket.

Savour.

LISA'S TIP

This recipe could be varied by using different honey choices. Try orange blossom, or flavour-infused honeys like lavender, rosemary, lemon or cinnamon. You can also drizzle over some balsamic glaze if you'd prefer.

Honey & Soy Baked Salmon

An ideal of introducing fish to the pickiest of eaters. If you like a bit of a kick, add a bit of lime juice and chilli flakes to the marinade.

....

{serves 4}

ingredients

4 salmon fillets, skin on

5 tbsp orange juice

5 tbsp acacia honey

4 ½ tbsp light soy sauce

1 tbsp minced fresh ginger

5 garlic gloves, crushed

1 tbsp sunflower oil

1 tsp sesame oil

salt and black pepper

garnish

250g buckwheat soba gluten-free noodles

sesame seeds

Preparation time - 30 mins, cooking time - 12 to 15 mins (20 mins well cooked)

Preheat the oven to 375°F, gas mark 5, 190°C (170°C fan-assisted).

In a small non-stick saucepan, pour in orange juice, honey, soy sauce, garlic and ginger. Heat gently over a medium heat, stirring only once, for approximately one minute, then remove and leave to cool completely. Now pass through a sieve and discard the garlic and ginger. In a large non-stick frying pan, heat the oils over a gentle heat, remove from the heat, place the salmon fillets in the pan, flesh side down, for 30 seconds. Flip over using kitchen tongs and place back on a medium heat to get the skin crispy (approx. 1-2 minutes) then remove from the heat and cool completely.

Season the flesh side with a touch of salt and black pepper. If you have time, marinate the salmon. When the fish is cold, place in a large freezer bag with half of the cooled marinade and chill for at least 30 minutes or overnight, turning the bag a couple of times. Line a baking tray with parchment paper or foil. Place the salmon fillets on the tray, and if you haven't marinated the fish, pour ½ of your marinade over the salmon fillets, keeping the remaining marinade in the non-stick saucepan.

Bake in the preheated oven for 15 minutes. Reduce to 12 minutes if you like your salmon slightly rare in the middle. Bring the reserved marinade to a light boil in the small saucepan over a medium heat, cook for 5 minutes or until slightly thickened and syrupy.

Cook the buckwheat soba noodles as directed on the packaging. When the salmon is cooked, remove from the oven tray and pour over the remaining marinade. Sprinkle with sesame seeds and serve with buckwheat soba gluten-free noodles.

LISA'S TIP

To avoid overcooking, remain close to your oven. Remove fish promptly when your timer goes off. If it looks almost or just barely done (just barely pink all the way through), you've timed things perfectly, as it will finish cooking outside the oven.

Roasted Aubergine with Tahini & Pomegranate

A beautiful dish which marries jewel-like pomegranate
seeds with the black skin of the aubergines.

....

{serves 4 - 6}

ingredients

3 large aubergines

2 tbsp toasted sesame seeds

½ pomegranate, deseeded

2 tbsp acacia honey mild & sweet

fresh coriander, handful

4 tbsp extra virgin olive oil

2 tsp sesame oil

sea salt and cracked black pepper

garlic granules

tahini dressing

3 tbsp tahini paste

3 tbsp cold water

squeeze of lemon

1 tsp garlic paste

Preparation time - 40 mins, cooking time - 50 to 60 mins

Preheat the oven to 350°F, gas mark 4, 180°C (160°C fan-assisted).

Wash and pat dry the aubergine, then cut in half lengthwise (keeping the stalk on).

With the tip of a knife, score the flesh deeply in a diamond criss-cross pattern by making five or six long cuts on the diagonal, cutting at a steep angle, and then rotating the eggplant to make another set of similar cuts (although do not cut through to the skin).

Brush both sides with the 2 tbsp extra virgin olive oil and sesame oil.

Put the aubergine cut-side facing up on a baking tray lined with parchment paper.

Season with sea salt, black pepper and garlic granules, place in the preheated oven and bake for 40-50 minutes.

Check often to make sure that they do not burn. If your aubergine still isn't tender all the way through, bake for a further 5-10 minutes, then proceed with the rest of the recipe.

Remove from the oven, drizzle with 2 tbsp extra virgin olive oil, then leave to cool.

To make the tahini paste mix either by hand or in mini food processor, add the tahini paste, water, lemon, garlic paste and season with salt.

On a larger platter place the roasted aubergines around the plate.

Spoon the tahini paste around the plate.

Drizzle acacia honey around the plate and over the aubergines.

Then garnish with the toasted sesame seeds, fresh coriander and pomegranate seeds.

LISA'S TIP

Aubergines have a wonderfully 'meaty' texture and can be roasted in their skins until charred, so the pulp can be removed and blended with other ingredients, such as lemon, tahini, and garlic, as in the Middle Eastern dish baba ghanoush or the similar Greek dish, melitzanosaltata.

Butternut Squash and Carrot Soup

A heavenly shade of orange, the true colour of autumn leaves,
the soup looks fabulous served in a 'squash bowl'.

{serves 8}

ingredients

2 large butternut squash, peeled
and cubed (keep seeds for roasting)

2 large echalions shallots, sliced

6 carrots, cubed

½ litre vegetable stock

½ litre chicken stock

½ litre boiling water

2 tbsp olive oil

sea salt

white pepper

garnish

chives

roasted butternut squash seeds (see
Lisa's tip for instructions)

coconut yogurt (coyo)

Preparation time - 30 mins, cooking time - 40 mins

In a large saucepan on medium heat, sauté the shallots in olive oil until translucent (approx. 5 minutes).

Add the cubed butternut squash, continue to sauté for 3 minutes then add the cubed carrots.

Season with sea salt and white pepper.

Add your vegetable, chicken stock and boiling water. Increase the heat and bring the soup to boil for 3-5 minutes.

Reduce the heat to medium and cook for 40 minutes (if you find there is a lot of broth on the top, using a large spoon you can skim this off).

Remove from the heat and cool slightly.

Using a hand-held blender, purée the soup in the pot, or purée in batches in a blender or food processor.

If the soup is too thick, add a little extra boiling water (almond milk or soya milk are also good choices).

Garnish with coconut yogurt, roasted butternut squash seeds and chives.

LISA'S TIP

To make the squash bowl, cut the butternut squash just beyond the bulbous part of the squash where it meets the neck. Using a spoon, scoop out the seeds. Rinse the seeds to remove fibres and also the inside of the bulbous part of the butternut squash. Pat dry with kitchen towel. Preheat the oven to 350°F, gas mark 4, 180°C (160°C fan-assisted). Line a baking tray with parchment paper, place the butternut squash and seeds on the tray, and drizzle olive oil over. Sprinkle with sea salt and cracked black pepper. Roast the butternut squash uncovered for 40-50 minutes, but remove the seeds after 20-25 minutes. Season with a little touch of salt while the seeds are cooling. The toasted seeds will keep for several months in a sealed container. Serve your soup in the squash and top with the roasted seeds! PS - You can eat the skin of the butternut squash, enjoy!

Sweet Potato Gratin

A healthier version of the classic potato gratin with the refreshing flavours of fresh coriander and coconut milk.

{serves 4}

ingredients

3 large sweet potatoes, peeled and sliced on a mandolin

2 onions, finely sliced

2 tbsp coconut oil

2 garlic cloves, crushed

1 large handful fresh coriander, finely chopped

2 tsp palm sugar

200ml coconut milk

60g medium cornmeal

sea salt, white pepper, black pepper

chilli flakes

Preparation time - 30 mins, cooking time - 60 mins

Preheat the oven to 375°F, gas mark 5, 190°C (170°C fan-assisted).

In a non-stick frying pan sauté the onions until soft and translucent, then season with salt, white pepper and chilli flakes.

Add the crushed garlic cloves, palm sugar and chopped coriander to the onions and continue to cook over a gentle heat, then set aside.

Slice sweet potatoes into thin slices using a mandolin or carefully with a knife.

In a 23cm circular or oval Pyrex dish, lay the sautéed onions around the base.

Cover with the sweet potatoes overlapping in a concertina, season with a little sea salt and black pepper as you layer each level.

Pour the coconut milk over the sweet potatoes, until covered.

In a small bowl season the medium cornmeal with sea salt and white pepper, then sprinkle over the sweet potatoes to cover the dish.

Bake, uncovered, for about 60 minutes, rotating the pan in the oven after 30 minutes to ensure uniform baking.

When the potatoes are tender and the topping is crisp and golden brown, remove from the oven and let sit for 2 to 3 minutes so the potatoes can absorb some extra liquid.

If your topping isn't crispy when about to serve, pop under the grill for 1-2 minutes, keeping an eye on it, so it doesn't burn.

LISA'S TIP

Serve hot or cold with fish, chicken or meat. Sprinkle with toasted chopped pecans for a seasonal garnish. Place chopped nuts in a dry, non-stick pan on medium-high heat. Stirring occasionally, toast the nuts until aromatic, approximately 2-3 minutes being careful not to burn.

Chicken & Sweet Corn Soup

An incredibly silky soup, which once again shows that you
don't have to give up your take-away favourites!

{serves 4 - 6}

ingredients

1 litre chicken stock

375g canned creamed style corn
(Green Giant brand preferred)

198g canned sweet corn, sieved
(Green Giant brand preferred)

2 tsp light soy sauce

2 tsp corn flour mixed with tbsp.
cold water

1 egg, lightly beaten

150g cooked chicken breast,
shredded (optional)

sea salt, white pepper if needed or
chicken stock powder

garnish

spring onion, sliced

light soy sauce

Preparation time - 20 mins, cooking time - 10 mins

Heat up the chicken stock in a large saucepan.

Add the creamed corn and sieved sweet corn.

In a small mixing bowl combine the corn flour with 2 tbsp cold
water and stir.

Add the light soy sauce to the chicken stock, continue stirring for
5 minutes.

Add the corn flour mixture to thicken soup and the shredded
chicken (if using), increase to medium/high heat and cook for a
further 5 minutes.

Take off the heat, and after 5 minutes, check for seasoning.

Gently beat the egg in a small bowl, using a fork gently swirl the
lightly beaten egg little by little in the soup through the fork's tines
– then stir the soup gently in a circular motion. This should yield
delicate egg strips which disperse throughout the soup.

Serve with a garnish of spring onion.

LISA'S TIP

*Sweet corn chicken soup is my favourite Chinese soup. It is one of
the simplest soup recipes that can be made at home, and I guarantee
you that this soup will give any good Chinese restaurant a run for its
money!*

Parsnips with Sesame & Honey

Small touches, such as toasted seeds, make a bigger
than expected difference to everyday vegetables.

....

{serves 4 - 6}

ingredients

6 parsnips, peeled, cut lengthways
into 4 to 6 strips

2 tbsp extra virgin olive oil

sea salt

black pepper

paprika

1-2 tbsp honey, acacia is best

sesame seeds, handful

Preparation time - 30 mins, cooking time - 40 to 45 mins

Preheat the oven to 375°F, gas mark 5, 190°C (170°C fan-assisted).

Line a large baking tray with parchment paper.

Toast the sesame seeds: heat a heavy bottom frying pan to hot but
not burning.

Add the sesame seeds to the dry, hot pan and gently swirl the pan
around until you notice the seeds starting to colour. Place on a
plate immediately. They will continue to cook even when off the
heat. Set aside.

Peel all the parsnips, and cut in half lengthways then each half either
into two or three strips depending on size (ensure all parsnips spears
are of a similar size).

Place the parsnips on your lined baking tray, season generously with
sea salt, black pepper and paprika.

Rub these seasonings into the parsnip then coat in olive oil.

Place in the pre-heated oven for 40 minutes, although keep an eye
on them, turning them over after the first 20 minutes.

After 40 minutes, drizzle the honey and cook for a further 5 minutes.

Remove and place on your serving platter or plates and sprinkle the
toasted sesame seeds over the top.

LISA'S TIP
*You can enjoy these parsnips cold too, chop them up in a salad, or add
them to a frittata.*

Aubergine Sauce with Courgette Spaghetti

Courgette spirals makes a surprisingly tasty alternative to pasta. This aubergine sauce can also be cooked separately and used as a side dish or as a topping for quinoa.

....

{serves 4 - 6}

ingredients

2 large aubergines, cut into small cubes (approx. 1cm)

2 brown onions, chopped finely

2 tbsp extra virgin olive oil

2 tsp bouillon powder

4 garlic gloves, crushed

2 tsp tomato purée

1 x 400ml tomato sauce either tinned or glass jarred

3 tsp sun-dried tomato paste

mixed herbs

garnish

6 large courgettes, made into spirals

parmesan cheese, grated

½ tbsp extra virgin olive oil (if sautéing the courgette spirals)

black pepper & sea salt

Preparation time - 40 mins, cooking time - 50 mins

Add the olive oil to a large non-stick frying pan over a medium to high heat. Fry the onions until translucent.

Add the cubed aubergines, and continue sautéing for a further 10 minutes until the aubergine starts to soften up.

Add the bouillon powder to the frying pan and continue to cook for a further 10 minutes. You will notice that the powder will draw the moisture from the aubergines.

Add the crushed garlic, black pepper and a little salt. Continue to sauté.

Reduce the heat then add the tomato purée and sun-dried tomato paste.

Add the tomato sauce, increase the heat until bubbling (continue stirring) then reduce to simmer and leave to cook for 30 minutes.

If your sauce reduces too much, you can add a little water.

Spiralise the courgette and either serve raw or you can pan fry in 1/2 tbsp extra virgin olive oil, seasoned with sea salt and black pepper for 2 to 3 minutes.

Serve immediately, sprinkled with grated parmesan and black pepper.

LISA'S TIP

If you don't have a spiraliser you can serve this sauce with your choice of gluten free pasta. Or, if you prefer, try it cold with a variety of dips and gluten-free crackers!

Horseradish Mashed Potato

An elegant accompaniment to
meat, poultry, game or fish.

....

{serves 4 - 6}

ingredients

1 kilo Maris Piper potatoes, approx.
4 or 5 large ones

3-4 tbsp coconut or olive oil

1 tbsp horseradish cream

salt and white pepper

Preparation time - 20 mins, cooking time - 20 mins

Cut your potatoes into quarters and place in a saucepan with cold salted water and bring to the boil. Boil the potatoes for 20 mins until soft. Check with a knife that they are ready, then drain.

Next place a sieve over a bowl and squeeze your potatoes through the sieve or a potato ricer to remove any lump and bumps.

Add your coconut or olive oil and season with salt & white pepper.

Finally add your horseradish cream, give a good stir.

LISA'S TIP

Why don't you try piping out the mashed potatoes through a piping bag with a fluted nozzle? Such a fun way to serve individual portions of mashed taters! If you are so inclined, you can make these ahead of time up to the point of piping them out. Just cover them and set in the refrigerator until you are ready then bake to re-heat before serving.

Lamb Tagine with Prunes, Almonds & Dates

An ideal dish for a family gathering. Prepare then place in the oven and spend time with your guests before serving! Consider a crunchy chopped salad of shredded carrots, onions, red cabbage, cucumber and ruby red pomegranate drizzled with olive oil and seasoned with sea salt, cracked pepper and lemon to accompany.

....

{serves 4 - 6}

ingredients

1.5kg lamb shoulder, deboned, well-trimmed, cut in 3cm cubes

2 tbsp olive oil

1 onion, finely chopped

1 red onion, finely chopped

2 garlic cloves

50g blanched almonds

1 cinnamon stick

250g pitted prunes

70g pitted dates, sliced

2 tbsp acacia honey

1 x 400g tin plum tomatoes, sieved to discard the seeds

2 tbsp Osem brand onion soup mix dissolved in 250-300ml boiling water

50ml pomegranate concentrate dissolved with 50ml boiling water

sea salt and freshly ground black pepper

1 tsp ground ginger

1 tsp ground coriander

2 tsp cinnamon

garnish

fresh coriander, a small bunch

serve with quinoa or wholegrain rice

Preparation time - 40 mins, cooking time - 1.5 to 2hrs

Preheat the oven to oven 325°F, gas mark 3, 180°C (160°C fan-assisted).

Place a 29cm casserole dish over the stove, gently heat the olive oil, and sauté the finely chopped onions until translucent.

Decant the onions to a mixing bowl.

In a separate large mixing bowl, add ground ginger, coriander, cinnamon, paprika, garlic granules and sea salt and black pepper.

Place the casserole dish back on the stove, and seal the lamb for 5 minutes, then spoon the lamb into the mixing bowl with the seasoning.

Coat the lamb in the seasoning then set aside.

Pour the sautéed onions back into the casserole dish on the heat, add the crushed garlic and sauté for a further 5 minutes.

Add the chopped dates, prunes and almonds to the onions.

Pour in the dissolved pomegranate concentrate, onion soup mix and then add the seasoned lamb and the cinnamon stick, cook for a further 2 minutes.

Sieve the canned plum tomatoes discarding the seeds. Place the juice of the tomatoes into a small mixing bowl, add the honey, combine together then pour over the lamb.

Bring the liquid to the boil, then reduce to medium/low heat.

Cover with a lid and place in the preheated oven and cook gently for 1.5-2 hours, check every 30 minutes.

After 1 hour, add the chick peas, continue cooking and reduce the oven temperature to 300°F, gas mark 2, 160°C (140°C fan-assisted).

Serve immediately with quinoa or wholegrain rice.

LISA'S TIP

This dish is so comforting. The dates and honey give a natural sweetness. Fruits are so special served in festive stews, making this dish the perfect centrepiece for any celebration or family gathering.

Chicken Tagine with Apricots & Ginger

For modern cooks, a tagine is low-and-slow stewing, with very little fat or liquid. The Moroccan, Tunisian and Algerian dishes that form the basis of tagine cuisine feature an abundance of 'warm' spices -- cinnamon, cumin, coriander -- along with garlic, onion, and sometimes lemon.

....

{serves 4 - 6}

ingredients

8 chicken thighs

2 tbsp olive oil

1 onion, finely chopped

1 tbsp ginger, peeled and grated

1-2 (depending on preference) red chillies, deseeded and finely chopped

1 cinnamon stick

250g ready to eat dried apricots

2 tbsp acacia honey

1 x 400g tin plum tomatoes, sieved to discard the seeds

2 tbsp Osem brand onion soup mix

200-250ml boiling water

sea salt and freshly ground black pepper

paprika

garlic granules

garnish

fresh coriander, a small bunch

quinoa, cooked

Preparation time - 30 mins, cooking time - 1.5 - 2hrs

Preheat the oven to oven 200°C/400°F/Gas 6 (180°C fan-assisted).

Rinse off the chicken under cold water, and remove any stray feathers, by scraping with a blade of a knife.

Place a large non-stick frying pan on the stove, together with a splash of olive oil. When the pan is hot, place the chicken in the pan and seal for approximately 2 minutes on each side until golden, then remove from the heat.

When the chicken has cooled down, season with a little sea salt, black pepper, paprika and garlic granules.

Place your casserole dish over the stove, gently heat the olive oil, and sauté the finely chopped onion until translucent.

Turn the heat down and add the chillies and grated ginger cook for a further 2 minutes.

Add the apricots together with the cinnamon stick, and continue to cook again for a further 2 minutes.

Dissolve the onion soup mix in 200ml boiling water, then pour into the casserole dish (You may need an extra 50ml, once the chicken has been added, to ensure there is enough liquid to cover the base of the casserole dish and submerge the apricots).

Add the seasoned chicken thighs and carefully baste over the juices.

Sieve the canned plum tomatoes, to discard the seeds, into a small mixing bowl. Add the honey, combine together then pour over the chicken.

Bring the liquid to the boil, then reduce to medium/low heat.

Cover with a lid and place in the preheated over and cook gently for 1.5-2 hours, check every 30 minutes.

Garnish with fresh coriander and serve with plain cooked quinoa.

LISA'S TIP

The advantage of this recipe is that you don't need a tagine or lots of time. After getting the apricots simmering, toss everything except the coriander into the casserole dish. After 1.5-2 hours in the oven, it is ready to serve on a bed of quinoa.

Aubergine and Autumn Vegetable Curry

Seek out small, slender aubergines for this recipe. With less seeds, they tend to be less bitter and become tender and sweet when cooked.

{serves 4 - 6}

ingredients

2 aubergines, medium, cut into 1.5cm cubes

1 butternut squash, cut into 1.5cm cubes

2 sweet potatoes, cut into 1.5cm cubes

2 carrots, cut into 1.5cm rounds

1 red onion, small, sliced into half moons

1 white onion, small, sliced into half moons

1 tin butter beans, drained

400ml coconut milk

300g tomato pasta sauce (smooth as possible)

½ litre chicken or vegetable stock

3 garlic gloves, crushed

2 tsp mild madras curry powder

2 tsp coconut sugar

2 tbsp coconut oil

sea salt & black pepper

garnish

wholegrain rice

fresh coriander

Preparation time - 40 mins, cooking time - 2 hours

Preheat the oven to 400°F, gas mark 6, 200°C (180°C fan-assisted).

Heat the oil in a large (29cm diameter) casserole dish on medium heat.

Add the onions and sauté until translucent approx. 5 minutes.

Add the aubergines, salt, pepper, tomato sauce and crushed garlic, mix well and cook for 2-3 minutes longer.

Add the remaining vegetables: butternut squash, sweet potato, carrots and butter beans.

Pour over the chicken or vegtable stock, followed by the coconut cream, keep on the stove for another 2-4 minutes until the stew comes to a boil.

Add the curry powder and coconut sugar.

Cover the pot and place in the centre of the oven for two hours. Check every 30 minutes and stir to ensure nothing gets stuck to the base of the dish. If you would like to keep the dish in the oven after two hours reduce the oven temperature to 300°F, gas mark 2, 150°C (130°C fan-assisted).

Serve with coconut wholegrain rice & freshly chopped coriander.

LISA'S TIP

Sweet potatoes are packed with beta-carotene and antioxidants. In fact, they have more beta-carotene than carrots! They also contain vitamins C, E, folate, thiamine, riboflavin, fibre and several minerals. Because of their lower glycemic index, they are a carbohydrate-friendly choice, too.

Bolognese with Spiralised Sweet Potato

My version of 'spag bol', this meat and potatoes dish is
deliciously filling and nutritionally balanced.

{serves 4 - 6}

ingredients

500g lean minced beef

2 echalions shallots or white
onions, finely chopped

120g button mushrooms, cut into
small cubes

2 x 400g cans plum tomatoes,
sieved (discard the pulp and pips)

Small handful of basil or dried
mixed herbs

2 tbsp olive oil

2 tbsp tomato purée

2 tsp Worcestershire sauce

2 tsp honey

3 garlic gloves, crushed

150ml white wine

garlic granules

sea salt

cracked black pepper

garnish

4 large sweet potatoes

olive oil

parmesan cheese, grated

sprigs of basil

Preparation time - 40 mins, cooking time - 45 to 60 mins

Heat a large non-stick saucepan or flame-proof casserole dish over a
high heat, then add the oil together with the shallots or onions and
sauté until soft and translucent approx. 3 mins.

Remove the pan from the heat. Add the crushed garlic and
Worcestershire sauce. Coat the onions well then add the minced
beef in several batches until the onions are blended into the meat.

Return to the heat and continue to stir over a medium/high heat
until browned. Break up any lumps with the back of a wooden
spoon. At this point, the mince will have changed colour from pink
to grey, to golden brown.

Add the mushrooms and continue to stir for 3 minutes then add the
tomato purée.

Make a well in the centre and pour in the wine. Continue to stir for
3 minutes until the wine has evaporated.

Add the basil leaves, if using or add dried herbs then pour over
the tomato sauce and then season with salt, black pepper, garlic
granules and honey.

Partly cover the pan, then simmer on a low heat for 45-60 minutes
until the mince is tender and surrounded with a rich thick sauce
(stir every 10 minutes).

Taste to check seasoning. Add salt and pepper if necessary, and once
cooked set aside.

Peel the sweet potatoes, and spiralise to get sweet potato pasta.

Place in a large wok/frying pan and sauté in a drizzle of olive oil for
3-4 minutes to lightly soften.

The spiralised pasta should have a bite to it so be sure not to overcook.

When you're ready to serve, heat up the sauce.

Garnish with basil and a sprinkle of parmesan cheese.

LISA'S TIP

*This meat sauce is a good recipe to freeze up to 3 months. Defrost
thoroughly, then return to a saucepan and reheat gently, bubble for 10
minutes and use in other recipes.*

Autumnal Macarons

Macarons have a smoother texture than the ones found in traditional bakeries and often feature a filling. I've suggested dates or chestnuts.

{makes 22}

ingredients

125g almond meal
150g pure icing sugar
100g egg whites (approx. 3 eggs)
60g coconut sugar
natural yellow colouring gel

choice of fillings

150g dates (stones removed)
8 tbsp almond milk
sea salt, pinch
or
150g chestnut spread, vanilla
8 tbsp almond milk
sea salt, pinch

Preparation time - 2 hours, cooking time - 20 to 25 mins

Preheat the oven to 375°F, gas mark 5, 190°C (170°C fan-assisted).

Line baking trays with double sheets of baking paper or use a silicone or macaron mat. Sift almond meal and icing sugar together; sift mixture twice more, then set aside. Beat egg whites until foamy; add your food colouring at this point. Continue beating on low speed, adding coconut sugar a tbsp at a time. Increase to high speed and beat until mixture forms glossy, stiff peaks. Fold in half the almond meal mixture. Repeat with second half. Using your spoon or spatula, swipe the mixture against the side of the bowl. Then scoop the batter from the bottom and plop it upside-down. This movement deflates the meringue. Repeat process until batter is runny, shiny and slowly slides the sides. Test by plopping a teaspoon of batter on a small plate. If the peak sinks back into the batter within 15 seconds, it is done.

Fill a piping bag with a 1cm round nozzle, and pipe rounds of batter onto your baking trays. Now, bang your trays against the counter to knock any air out of the batter. Set aside to dry at room temperature for 45mins - 1 hour.

Place tray in the oven, reduce temperature to 140°C (120°C fan-assisted). Bake for 20-25 minutes. Watch that your macarons don't burn. They are ready when they can be lifted from the baking paper without sticking. Mine usually take 23 minutes but this may vary.

To make the date or chestnut filling, place the dates or chestnut spread in a mini food processor blend until smooth and then add the almond milk and pinch of sea salt blending until smooth. Place the filling on one macaron then cover with another one.

Heaven.

LISA'S TIP

Every baker has an opinion about the best way to create the perfect macaron batter, a process known as macaronnage. The idea is to press out just enough air from the batter so that it runs off your spatula thickly, slowly, but consistently.

Apple & Almond Pudding

Comfort food can look appealing, too. Prepare in ramekins
and serve individually for a more sophisticated look.

{serves 4 - 6}

ingredients

700g cooking apples, cored, peeled
and roughly chopped

150ml water, just enough to cover
the apples)

2 tbsp honey, depending on the
sharpness of the apples

120g coconut sugar

120g ground almonds, sieved

120g margarine

2 large eggs, beaten

garnish

coconut yogurt (coyo)

Preparation time - 30 mins, cooking time - 30 to 40 mins

Preheat the oven to 375°F, gas mark 5, 180°C (160°C fan-assisted).

Core, peel and roughly chop the cooking apples.

Place in a saucepan with approximately 150ml water, just enough
to cover the apples, together with 2 tbsp honey (depending on the
sharpness of the apples).

Bring to a boil then cook over a low heat until the apples are stewed,
approx. 10 minutes.

Remove from heat and allow to cool for 10 minutes, then transfer
into an 18cm Pyrex bowl.

Using an electric mixer or by hand, cream the margarine and
coconut sugar until pale and fluffy. Then beat in the eggs a little at
a time.

When both eggs are incorporated, carefully and lightly fold in the
sieved ground almonds.

Spread this mixture carefully over the apples, and even out the
surface with the back of a tablespoon.

Bake on a middle shelf for 30-40 minutes.

Serve hot or cold with coconut yogurt.

LISA'S TIP

*Can also be served with banana ice cream. Once cooled, it will keep in
the fridge up to 4 days. You can also try different variations of fruits:
rhubarb, plum, peaches, apricot or pear! This is a perfect dessert for
guests who are wheat or gluten intolerant.*

Raw Chocolate Brownies

Made with whole food ingredients, these
divine brownies are truly indulgent.

{makes 16 squares}

ingredients

250g rolled jumbo oats (gluten-free
if required), blended
500g pitted Medjool soft dates
25g raw cacao powder
½ tsp pure vanilla bean extract
¼ tsp sea salt, crushed
100g dark chocolate chips (or you
can use milk chocolate chips if no
dairy allergies)

chocolate coating

160g sunflower oil or (coconut oil
if no nut allergies)
120g agave nectar or maple syrup
80g cocoa powder
sea salt
1 tsp pure vanilla bean extract

Preparation time - 30 mins, freeze time - 30 mins (plus refrigeration)

Line a 23cm square pan with parchment paper.

In a food processor, process the oats into a fine sandy consistency
with slight rough texture.

Add the pitted dates and process until finely chopped and smooth.

Add the cacao powder, vanilla, and sea salt and process until
thoroughly combined, keep scraping down the sides, and breaking
up the mixture.

When the mixture has formed into a log or ball shape remove from
the food processor and place in your pre-lined tin.

I wear disposable gloves at this point to evenly press the mixture
into the prepared square pan until smooth, or you can use the back
of a large spoon.

Then scatter over the chocolate chips and then press into the
mixture.

Place in the freezer for about 10 minutes.

For the chocolate topping: pour the sunflower/coconut oil into a
mixing bowl and add the following ingredients: cacao powder,
syrup, salt, and vanilla and whisk until combined and smooth.

Remove the brownies from the freezer and pour on the chocolate
topping and spread out evenly.

Carefully transfer the pan to the freezer on a flat even surface and chill
for 20 or more minutes or until the topping is firm enough to slice.

Run hot water over a knife for a minute or so, wipe quickly with
a towel, and carefully slide the knife into the brownies to slice
(warming up the knife helps it slice more evenly without much
cracking).

Store leftovers in the fridge for a chocolate treat anytime!

Invite friends round to share!

LISA'S TIP

*You have to keep these brownies either in the freezer or fridge to prevent
the topping from melting, however remove from the fridge or freezer 30
minutes before serving. My advice would be, once made, cut into squares
and keep on a flat platter covered with cling film in the fridge.*

Fig & Almond Cake

This is a light cake that's rich and buttery on the bottom. An ideal treat that has the health benefits of almonds and figs.

{serves 10 - 12}

ingredients

3-4 fresh figs, sliced thinly (remove base and stalk)
4 large eggs
228g margarine
228g coconut sugar
228g ground almonds, sifted
½ tsp almond extract

topping

20g flaked almonds, toasted
2 tbsp apricot or strawberry jam (sugar free)

Preparation time - 20 mins, cooking time - 45 mins

Preheat the oven to 375°C, gas mark 5, 180°C (160°C fan-assisted).

Line the base and side of a non-stick, loose bottom, 20cm springform tin with parchment paper.

Place the sliced figs around the base of the tin.

In an electric mixer or by hand, cream the margarine and coconut sugar until pale and fluffy. Now beat in the eggs a little at a time.

Add the almond extract and then lightly fold in the sieved ground almonds.

Spread this mixture carefully over the figs, and even out the surface with the back of a tablespoon.

Then bake on a middle shelf in the oven for exactly 45 minutes.

Remove from the oven and leave to cool over a wire rack.

When cooled, loosen the cooked mixture around the edges.

Place a serving plate over the tin and flip over, then release the clasp.

Peel away the parchment paper.

For the apricot or strawberry glaze: heat the jam in a small saucepan over a medium heat until liquid (melted). You can add a touch of water if the consistency is too thick. Then remove from the heat and strain the jam through a fine strainer to remove any fruit lumps, let cool until it is only slightly warm, then using a pastry brush glaze the tart.

Sprinkle with toasted almonds.

Serve with ice cream or coconut yogurt.

LISA'S TIP

The cake itself is simple to make and very good! Consider using apricots or peaches instead of figs. Store in an airtight container in the fridge for up to 5 days. Bring to room temperature before serving.

WINTER

seasonal moods

Diffused light makes our landscapes softer and if it snows, there's a quiet like no other time. Our tendency is to run from work to home, escaping the cold and rushing inside, but when there's a clear winter day, there are few things more beautiful. We just have to remember to look!

While the trees might be bare of their leaves, the ground is active. Now is when root vegetables are at their peak: celeriac with its distinctive flavour and versatile uses; sensational beetroot with its sultry red colour and taste; and Jerusalem artichokes which add a nutty flavour to soups. Brussels sprouts, when prepared with love and time, are surprisingly delicious as is spinach, perhaps flavoured with lemon, a taste of forgotten sun.

Inside the house – and perhaps just a little too close to the kitchen – temptations are plenty. Use the weather to your advantage and keep your house full of delicious, attractive choices in brilliant colours. Make larger quantities of soups, stews and casseroles to share - after all, what's really better than providing healthy, nourishing foods to those we love?

BEETROOT The Romans praised its medicinal and aphrodisiac qualities, but beetroots are a new superfood because of an abundance of potassium and magnesium. Roast them for an added depth of flavour.

JERUSALEM ARTICHOKE
Related to the sunflower and not a true artichoke, this oddly named tuber has a sweet nutty flavour. Traditionally used in soups, it is high in iron and vitamin C. But, beware, it does have a property similar to baked beans!

PISTACHIOS With fewer calories than the average nut, pistachios are also a rich source for potassium and vitamin K. Grown in dry Mediterranean climates and recently cultivated in California, pistachios can be used in both sweet and savoury dishes.

SPINACH Belonging to the food group family that also includes beetroot, chard and quinoa, spinach has an impressive array of health benefits. It contains vitamin C, vitamin E, beta-carotene, manganese, zinc and selenium. Try steamed, sautéed or raw in salads.

CARROTS While seeing in the dark is a myth, carrots do contain the highest level of vitamin A found in a vegetable. Try tossing them in cider vinegar for an energising salad or, like other root vegetables, they benefit from roasting.

CELERIAC A singularly unattractive vegetable, celeriac is ideal for low-carbohydrate diets. Chip, mash or grate for a huge variety of delicious variations. A French-staple which is slowly making its way into mainstream meals, celeriac tastes like a cross between potatoes and celery.

LEMON Natural vitamin C is much more effective than synthetic, so reduce your chances of catching a cold by drinking some fresh lemon juice diluted in water every day. Try hot water with a touch of honey and lemon for a refreshingly warm variation.

BRUSSELS SPROUTS One of the world's healthiest foods (really!), this edible bud packs in over 100% of your daily requirement of vitamin C. Low in fat and sodium the mighty sprout needs a delicate hand. Try cutting them in half, blanching, then tossing in olive oil and garlic. Delicious!

Omelette with Avocado & Sunkissed Tomato

A quick, nutritious breakfast that also works well in the
evening with a green salad and a glass of wine!

{serves 2}

ingredients

6 eggs
2 tbsp coconut oil
sea salt and white pepper

garnish

1 avocado, cut each half in six slices
1 medium tomato, cut into 6 wedges
8 sunkissed tomatoes
1 handful fresh coriander, chopped
balsamic, drizzle
olive oil
cracked black pepper

Preparation time - 15 mins, cooking time - 3 mins per omelette

To cook the omelette, preheat a 7cm non-stick pan over a medium to high heat.

Beat the eggs with a fork until they are well blended with no streaks of egg white. Season with salt and white pepper.

Add the coconut oil to the pan, once melted, turn the heat down to medium.

Add the eggs and scramble with a heat-resistant spatula. Once the eggs begin to set a bit, shake the pan back and forth while still scrambling, so the runny egg fills any gaps or holes on the bottom.

Once the egg has almost set, turn down the heat to medium/low and evenly smooth out.

Now slide onto a serving plate. Top with avocado slices, tomato wedges, sunkissed tomatoes.

Season with sea salt and cracked black pepper.

Lightly drizzle with olive oil and balsamic.

Omelettes are very filling although you can serve with some gluten-free bread to mop up any juices!

LISA'S TIP

If you prefer you can add filling directly onto the omelette in the pan. The number one rule is not to over-mix – no beating or whisking. Practice with plain omelettes before you try filling. Don't put too much inside; it gets difficult to fold the omelette over. You can always put more filling on top.

Green Goddess Smoothie

This Green Goddess smoothie is great for balancing sugar cravings, uplifting the mood, clearing the head, boosting metabolism and strengthening immunity.

{serves 2}

ingredients

400ml apple juice

1 large banana, frozen if you prefer ice cold smoothies

1 kiwi

½ cucumber, peeled and cut into chunks

½ avocado

1 inch ginger, peeled and grated

1 large handful curly kale, stalks removed or spinach

1 bunch of fresh coriander

1 tbsp SuperLife Superfood smoothie mix

couple of ice cubes if you are using fresh bananas

garnish

cucumber slices

fresh coriander

Preparation time - 20 mins

Peel and slice: kiwi, avocado, cucumber and your banana if not already frozen.

Peel and grate the ginger finely.

In a blender, combine the apple juice, banana, kiwi, avocado and cucumber and blend until smooth.

Add the ginger, curly kale or spinach and coriander, and again thoroughly blend.

Add the SuperLife Superfood smoothie mix and ice cubes if required and give one more blend again till smooth.

Divide between two tall glasses or mason jars and serve right away, or you can keep refrigerated, for one day.

Drink and feel great.

LISA'S TIP

SuperLife Smoothie Mix is a combination of eight raw superfoods that gives you an energy boost for the entire day.
1. Hemp - rich in protein and omega-3s
2. Maca - for energy, focus & memory, and an aphrodisiac
3. Lucuma - balances sugar levels for lasting energy
4. Cacao - high in magnesium, energy & mood booster
5. Spirulina - anti-inflammatory, strengthens the joints
6. Chlorella - strengthens immune system, helps remove toxins
7. Kelp - high in iodine, balances thyroid
8. Barley Grass - high in chlorophyll, alkalizes the body, helps with weight loss.

Eggs Baked in Portobello Mushrooms

This breakfast dish can also be served with rocket and
sunkissed tomatoes for a lunchtime treat.

{serves 4}

ingredients

4 portobello mushrooms, insides
scraped and stalks

4 eggs, medium

olive oil

sea salt and

black pepper

4 tbsp grated mozzarella

3 tbsp finely grated parmesan
cheese

garnish

2 avocados, cubed

3-4 medium tomatoes, deseeded
and chopped into chunks

1-2 tbsp sweet chilli sauce

1 tbsp olive oil

fresh coriander, chopped, about a
handful

chives, chopped

Preparation time - 20 mins, cooking time - 14 to 15 mins

Preheat the oven to 350°F, gas mark 4, 180°C (160°C fan-assisted).

Line a baking tray with parchment paper.

Clean the mushrooms with a mushroom brush.

Carefully cut out the stalk, then with a teaspoon scoop out the gills
of each portobello mushroom cap. This will give you extra room
and prevent your mushroom from being too watery.

Place the mushrooms on the baking tray, drizzle a teaspoon of olive
oil, then season with a little sea salt and black pepper.

In a separate small bowl, crack each egg then pour into the
mushroom cap.

Sprinkle a little pinch of salt over the egg, 1 tbsp of mozzarella
around the white of the egg, and scatter over the parmesan cheese,
leaving some of the yolk exposed.

Bake in the preheated oven on the centre shelf for 14-15 minutes.

To make the avocado salsa, mix the cubed avocado, tomato and
season with sea salt, black pepper, olive oil, chopped coriander and
sweet chilli sauce.

Remove baked eggs from oven and allow to set for about 3 minutes
before serving.

Scatter the avocado & tomato salsa over the baked eggs and garnish
with chopped chives.

Winter

192

LISA'S TIP

*Since this recipe is so quick to pull together and packed with tons of
flavour and nutrition, you'll turn to it time and again.*

Homemade Granola

This homemade granola allows you to control the amount of sugar on your morning cereal. The freshly roasted nuts add flavour to a higher level, too!

{serves 12}

ingredients

400g gluten-free oats, sifted
60g sunflower seeds
60g pumpkin seeds
80g whole pecans
100g whole almonds
4 tbsp rice bran oil
8 tbsp maple syrup
2 pinches sea salt
1 tsp vanilla bean extract

garnish

1 tbsp toasted sesame seeds
100g raisins
80g banana chips
20g coconut chips

Preparation time - 20 mins, cooking time - 15 to 20 mins

Preheat the oven to 400°F, gas mark 6, 200°C (180°C fan-assisted).

Cover a large baking tray with parchment paper, add the sifted oats, whole almonds, whole pecans, sunflower and pumpkin seeds and spread in a even layer.

Bake in the preheated oven for 10 minutes, check every 5 minutes and stir to ensure the nuts don't over brown or burn.

Bake until crisp and golden.

In a small sauce pan heat the oil, maple syrup, vanilla bean extract and salt over a gentle heat for 2 minutes, then set aside.

When the oat mixture has cooked, remove from the oven and pour over the maple syrup mixture, mix until well coated.

Reduce the oven temperature to 275°F, gas mark 1, 140°C (120°C fan-assisted).

Place the granola back in the oven, cook for 5-10 minute, stirring after 5 minutes.

Remove from the oven and leave to cool on the tray, add the toasted sesame seeds, banana & and raisins.

Serve with cold milk or yogurt.

The granola can be stored in an airtight container for up to a month.

LISA'S TIP

Serve on coconut yogurt, topped with granola and blueberries. You can be adventurous with your nuts and seeds. When cooked you can add an assortment of dried fruits. My preference is for dried banana chips and pecans, but once you get the hang of making your own, you really can be adventurous!

Roasted Beetroot & Orange Salad

Not only is this an attractive dish, the
'sugared' walnuts are addictive – beware!

{serves 4}

ingredients

720g beetroots (approximately 4 large beetroots) trimmed and scrubbed

3 large oranges, pith and peel removed and cut into segments (see Lisa's tip)

100g stilton cheese, crumbled

80g walnuts

boiling water

1 tbsp coconut sugar

3 tbsp extra virgin olive oil

sea salt and cracked black pepper

garnish

garnish with some rocket, chopped chives, coriander or parsley

Preparation time - 20 mins, cooking time - 1 hour plus cooling time

Preheat the oven to 400°F, gas mark 6, 200°C (180°C fan-assisted).

To roast the beetroots, if the leaves are still attached, cut them off, leaving 1 inch of the stem attached, scrub with cold water but do not peel. Place 4 squares of aluminium foil on a baking tray enough to cover the beetroots and make into a parcel. Placing the beetroot on each, lift the corners to cover, then divide 1 tbsp of extra virgin olive oil between the 4 parcels, wrap tightly, pinching the edges of the foil together. Place in the preheated oven for about 1 hour, or until tender when pierced with a thin knife or a skewer. When fully roasted, remove and carefully open the foil packet. Let the beetroots stand until cool enough to handle. Now while wearing rubber gloves, place the beetroot in your hand and carefully peel off the outer layer. Cut the beetroots into chunky slices, place in a mixing bowl and season with sea salt and cracked black pepper, drizzle with 2 tbsp extra virgin olive oil.

Bring a small saucepan of water to the boil, add the walnuts and boil for 2 minutes, then strain through a sieve. Place on a baking tray with parchment paper and toss the nuts in coconut sugar. Bake in the oven for 8-10 minutes. Segment the oranges (see Lisa's tip).

Place the beetroots on a serving platter, again using rubber gloves, then top with the orange segments, crumbled blue cheese and toasted sugared walnuts. If you desire, drizzle with olive oil and season with a little sea salt and black pepper. Garnish with some rocket, chopped chives, coriander or parsley.

LISA'S TIP

The trick to segmenting oranges is to cut the ends off an orange just far enough to expose the flesh, then place the orange cut end down, and cut away as little of the peel as possible by following the orange's shape. Using a sharp knife cut along the inside of the membranes that separate the orange segments, slice only down to the center of the orange, continue around entire orange cutting out each section, leaving the membrane.

Courgette & Shiitake Mushroom Quinoa Frittata

Frittatas are Italian, open-faced omelettes traditionally started on the stove and finished under the grill. Use any combination of vegetables for good results.

{serves 8 - 10}

ingredients

150g quinoa
250ml cold water
300g shiitake mushrooms, sliced
6 large eggs, beaten
2 courgettes, grated
2 tbsp coconut oil
150g grated cheddar cheese
2 tbsp honey
2 tbsp soy sauce, light
sea salt and white pepper

Preparation time - 30 mins, cooking time - 50 to 55 mins

Preheat the oven to 350°F, gas mark 4, 180°C (160°C fan-assisted)

Line the base and sides of a 23cm non-stick springform tin with parchment paper.

Place the quinoa in a sieve and rinse until the water runs clear. Place in a medium saucepan with 250ml cold water and bring to a boil. Cover and simmer for 15 minutes, then take off the heat and leave to cool.

In a frying pan, add the coconut oil and sauté the sliced mushrooms until soft. Now add the soy sauce and honey, and continue to cook for 5 minutes. Leave to cool.

In a large mixing bowl, add the eggs and beat well, season with sea salt and white pepper.

Add the grated courgette, grated cheese, quinoa and mushrooms and mix well.

Place the tin over a tray with a rack underneath to prevent any leakage from the tin. Pour the mixture in the prepared tin.

Cover with foil and bake for 30 minutes, then remove the foil and bake for a further 20 minutes uncovered until golden and crisp. You might need an extra 5 minutes.

Leave to cool then release the side of the tin and you're ready to serve!

LISA'S TIP

This recipe is so versatile, and perfect for picnics or lunches on the move. I tend to have one of these quinoa frittata cakes sitting in my fridge each week as a slice is healthy snack between meals. This recipes contains fresh courgette, shiitake mushrooms and cheddar cheese, because that's what I had in the fridge, but I can think of a million different combos that would be equally delish; broccoli & cheddar, sundried tomato & pesto, butternut squash & feta. Or grated sweet potato and courgette, and just don't forget to add the honey and soy to this combination. The possibilities are endless!

Moroccan Carrot & Chickpea Quinoa Salad

If you want even more Moroccan flavour, add cumin to the
quinoa when cooking or rosewater to the cooled dish.

....

{serves 6 - 8}

ingredients

240g quinoa, mixed red and white

4 carrots, grated

100g raisins

1 tsp olive oil

1 tsp cinnamon

2 tsp acacia honey

½ litre boiling water

120g chickpeas, rinsed

2 handfuls, chopped coriander

2 tbsp olive oil

3 tsp lemon juice

sea salt and black pepper

paprika

garnish

20g crushed pistachios

35g toasted pine nuts

fresh coriander to taste or flat-leaf
parsley

Preparation time - 30 mins, cooking time - 25 mins

In a medium saucepan, add the 1 tsp olive oil. Add the grated carrots
and raisins and sauté over a gentle heat.

Add the quinoa, cinnamon and honey, then stir till thoroughly
combined.

Add the boiling water, bring back to the boil, then cover. Reduce the
heat to a simmer and cook for 20 minutes. Remove from the heat
and let the mixture rest for a further 5 minutes.

Fluff with a fork then leave to cool.

Toast the pine nuts in a non-stick pan over a medium heat until
browned.

In a large mixing bowl, add: 2 tbsp olive oil, lemon juice, chickpeas,
coriander, salt, pepper and paprika.

When the quinoa has fully cooled, fold it into the mixture in the
large mixing bowl.

Scatter with toasted pine nuts and crushed pistachios.

Garnish with freshly chopped coriander or flat-leaf parsley.

LISA'S TIP

*Sometimes 'cupboard cooking' yields fantastic results. This recipe was
invented when I needed to use up a bunch of fresh herbs and some
canned chickpeas I had on hand. Now, my family requests the dish!
This salad will keep for a few days in the fridge, during which time
the flavours can often improve.*

Petit Pois, Avocado & Crispy Curly Kale Salad

Striking colours and bold flavours
makes this salad a real winner!

....

{serves 4-6}

ingredients

300g petit pois, frozen (thawed)

100g curly kale

2 avocados cut into small cubes

300g beetroots, rinse under water before roasting leave the skin on

bunch of chives

sea salt and

cracked black pepper

chilli flakes

4 tbsp extra virgin olive oil

dressing

100ml extra virgin olive oil

20ml white wine vinegar

25ml balsamic

1tsp Dijon honey mustard

1 ¼ tbsp acacia honey

Preparation time - 60 mins, cooking time - 30 mins

Preheat the oven to 375°F, gas mark 5, 190°C (170°C fan-assisted)

Remove the petit pois from the freezer and leave in a bowl to thaw out.

Make the dressing by mixing together with a small whisk: extra virgin olive oil, white wine vinegar, balsamic, Dijon honey mustard, honey, and sea salt and black pepper.

Place each beetroot on individual large square of foil. Pick up the sides and meet at the top to create a parcel. Drizzle inside each parcel with olive oil and season with sea salt, cracked black pepper and chilli flakes.

Close the parcels and place on a baking tray for 40-50 minutes until soft.

Remove from oven and leave to cool, before peeling off the skin.

Once completely cooled, gently rub off the skins (best to wear disposable gloves)

Cut into small cubes, then pour 2 tbsp of the dressing and leave to marinade.

Line a baking tray with parchment paper. Place the curly kale on the tray and drizzle over the leaves with olive oil, a sprinkle of cracked pepper and sea salt. Toss to coat completely.

Bake until the edges are brown but not burnt, about 8-10 minutes.

You can take the tray out after 5 minutes and turn over the leaves with a spatula if the edges are browning too quickly. It is done when the kale is crispy, not soft.

In a mixing bowl, add the petit pois, avocado and chopped chives. Lightly stir together, then place on a large serving platter and drizzle with 1 tbsp of the dressing.

Using gloves, carefully place the cubed beetroot over the peas and avocado, reserving any juices. Top the salad with the crispy, curly kale.

Drizzle around the plate with any juices from the beetroot.

LISA'S TIP

Kale is one of the most nutritionally rich vegetables grown in Britain, and with its curly leaves it's also one of the most attractive. So it's a mystery as to why it remains so underused by today's consumers. Don't miss out on this delicious 'superfood' - try it today!

Salmon with Wasabi Mayonnaise & Pistachio Crust

A quick, mid-week meal or formal enough for a dinner party,
this dish works well with a cucumber and dill salad.

{serves 4}

ingredients

4 salmon fillets, approximately
550g (with skin)

1 tsp sesame oil

½ tbsp sunflower oil

1 tbsp mayonnaise

½ tsp wasabi powder/paste

40g roughly chopped pistachios

sea salt

cracked black pepper

Preparation time - 20 mins, cooking time - 10 to 12 mins (15 minutes if well cooked)

Preheat the oven to 400°F, gas mark 6, 200°C (180°C for fan-assisted). Wash and pat dry the salmon fillets.

In a large non-stick frying pan, heat the sunflower and sesame oil and place the salmon fillets in the pan, flesh side down, for 20 seconds.

Turn the fillets over onto the skin side and cook for 2 minutes over a medium high heat. Take off the heat and allow to cool.

Once cooled, season the fillets with salt and cracked black pepper.

Mix 1 tsp mayonnaise with ¼ tsp of wasabi powder or paste.

Place the fillets on a greased baking tray or dish, or if your frying pan can go in the oven, then use the same frying pan.

Using a knife, spread the mayonnaise mixture evenly over the top over the four fillets.

Press the chopped pistachios onto the top of each fillet covering completely.

Bake salmon until cooked through and the nut topping is crisp and golden brown, about 10-12 minutes (cook for 15 minutes if you prefer well cooked).

Using a large spatula, transfer salmon fillets onto a platter.

LISA'S TIP

It used to be seen as a luxury but now salmon is one of the most popular oily fish consumed in the UK. And why not when it's so versatile, readily available and is in season right now. If your pocket can afford it, wild salmon is worth seeking out rather than the farmed variety which can be fatty and tasteless. While many people find the stronger flavours of mackerel or sardines too much, salmon is a fantastic oily fish to include in your diet for wonderful health benefits.

Brussels Sprout Chips

Wait, don't turn the page – these chips are crispy, salty
and have an abundance of Vitamin C.

{serves 4 - 6}

ingredients

400g Brussels sprouts, stems
removed and leaves separated

10g parmesan cheese, grated

1 tbsp olive oil

sea salt

black pepper

paprika

Preparation time - 20 mins, cooking time - 18 to 20 mins

Preheat the oven to 375°F, gas mark 5, 190°C (170°C fan-assisted)

Wash Brussels sprouts, trim the bottom stems and discard.

Remove any wilted outer leaves and discard.

Cut each sprout in half, remove loose leaves.

Combine halves and leaves in a bowl and toss with olive oil, salt, pepper and paprika.

Place on a foil-lined baking sheet and bake 10 minutes stirring every few minutes to prevent burning.

Now add the grated parmesan cheese and bake for a further 8-10 minutes.

Now, aren't you glad you didn't turn the page?

LISA'S TIP

The easiest way to release the leaves is to keep trimming the bottom stem as you peel away the layers. This is the most time consuming part, but once it is done, the rest is a breeze. If you find peeling the layers off too time consuming, you can simply cut in half through the stem and roast the same way, although you might need to increase the cooking time by 5-10 minutes. Top the roasted Brussels sprout chips with extra parmesan, and this is one addictive snack!

Borscht Soup

This soup from Eastern Europe has become trendy again. Perhaps more people are becoming aware of the health benefits of beets?

....

{serves 8 - 10}

ingredients

1.3k large beetroots, peeled, skinned and cut into 3cm strips

1 large onion, sliced

2 celery stalks, cut into 3 pieces

2 carrots, cut in half lengthways and then into 3 pieces

2 tbsp vegetable oil

2 tbsp chicken stock powder

2 tbsp vegetable bouillon powder

4 pints water

2 tbsp acacia honey

2 tbsp sushi season vinegar

sea salt

white pepper

garnish

sour cream or coconut cream

fresh chopped dill leaves

whole beetroot from soup

grated hard boiled eggs

boiled potatoes

Preparation time - 30 mins, cooking time - 45 mins plus cooling and chilling time

Wearing gloves, trim the beetroots, wash then peel the skins and cut into 3cm strips, so you have thick matchstick pieces (try to make as equal sizes, then you can use in a salad or as garnish).

Prepare the other vegetables as stated.

In a large saucepan on a high heat, add the vegetable oil and sauté the onions until soft.

Then add the carrots and celery and continue to sauté. Add the chicken and vegetable powder, and keep stirring.

Remove from the heat and add the beetroot. Then place back on the heat and add a little over 2 litres of boiling water.

Season with sea salt and white pepper. Then add the honey.

Bring to boil then cover loosely and continue to cook on a medium heat for 45 minutes.

After 45 minutes, remove from the heat and add the sushi seasoning vinegar.

Leave to cool completely for 3-4 hours.

Now place a large sieve over another large saucepan and strain through your soup.

Discard the celery stalk and keep the cooked beetroot and carrots.

Once the soup has cooled completely, place in the fridge until nice and cold.

When ready to serve, garnish with the reserved beetroot, chopped boiled eggs, boiled cubed potatoes, fresh dill leaves and coconut or sour cream.

LISA'S TIP

I used fresh beets from my local 'pick your own'. I love the deep ruby color of this borscht! It's so healthy and nutritious. It's as authentic as it gets. It can be served vegetarian style by omitting the chicken stock powder and doubling up on the bouillon.

Spicy Potatoes

Serve these spicy potatoes as part of an Indian buffet or liven
up your weekend roast with these crunchy firecrackers!

{serves 4-6}

ingredients

1.2 kg Maris Piper potatoes
4 tbsp peanut or coconut oil
1 tsp black mustard seeds
1 tsp cumin seeds
½ tsp ground cumin
½ tsp sweet paprika
1 ½ tsp turmeric
¼ tsp chilli flakes
1 clove garlic crushed
2 tbsp lemon juice
salt

Preparation time - 30 mins, cooking time - 40 to 50 mins

Preheat the oven to 180 °C

Cut your potatoes in half, then quarter, then quarter each quarter
again, and boil until just tender, approx. 10 -12 mins. Rinse under
cold water, drain and cool.

Combine potatoes, peanut oil, seeds, spices, salt, garlic and lemon
juice in a baking dish.

Cook in hot oven for about 30-40 minutes or until potatoes are nice
and crispy.

LISA'S TIP

*This recipe can be made 3 hours ahead. Store it, covered, in your
refrigerator. It can also be eaten cold. Just stir in 1 tbsp of coconut
cream with chopped coriander and 1 tbsp mango chutney for a
different style potato salad.*

Sweet Potato Hummus

An exciting version of this Middle Eastern dip
which also features pine nuts for crunch.

{serves 8 - 10}

ingredients

2 x 400g tins chickpeas in water,
drained

1 whole lemon

6-8 tbsp extra virgin olive oil

4 tbsp raw tahini

3 garlic gloves crushed

4 tbsp water

sea salt

1 large sweet potato, roasted in skin

garnish

paprika

2 tbsp chickpeas

olive oil

toasted pine nuts

parsley, Italian flat-leaf, roughly
chopped

Preparation time - 30 mins, cooking time - 50 to 60 minutes

Preheat the oven to 400°F, gas mark 6, 200°C (180°C fan-assisted)
Place the large sweet potato on a baking tray and bake for 50-60
minutes until soft, then remove from the oven and leave to cool.

Place the chickpeas in the food processor, reserving 2 tbsp for the
garnish. Add 4 tbsp of tahini and process until smooth, occasionally
wiping down the sides.

Add the crushed garlic, lemon juice, water, 6 tbsp olive oil and salt
and process.

You may need to add 3 tbsp olive oil. Taste and adjust the seasoning.

If the paste is too thick, add 2-3 tbsp of water.

Scoop the inside of the sweet potato out of the skin and blend again
until smooth.

To serve, place in serving dishes, using the back of a spoon create
a well, drizzle with olive oil, sprinkle with the rest of the chickpeas,
paprika, toasted pine nuts and chopped parsley.

LISA'S TIP

*Hummus, the Arabic word for 'chickpeas', is relatively easy to make
with the help of a blender and a few common, inexpensive ingredients.
There are several brands of sesame tahini available and the one you
choose can dramatically change the flavour of your hummus. Raw
tahini can give your hummus a stronger and bitter flavour while
canned, roasted tahini is mild and nutty.*

Jerusalem Artichoke Soup

A good way to finally try those 'funny-looking' vegetables. A truly warming and satisfying soup with the added bonus of a crispy parsnip topping.

{serves 4 - 6}

ingredients

1 kg Jerusalem artichokes, peeled and cut into 4 cm pieces

960ml, boiling water

2 echalion shallots, finely sliced (or 4 shallots)

2 tsp bouillon

3 tbsp olive or rice bran oil

2 cloves garlic, peeled

2 parsnips, peel and cut into 2 cm pieces

1 tbsp coconut yogurt (if needed)

sea salt & white pepper

garnish

2 parsnips, peeled with vegetable peeler

300ml sunflower oil for frying

Preparation time - 30 mins, cooking time - 30 mins

Heat the oil in a heavy saucepan and sauté the finely sliced shallots until translucent.

Add the garlic and sauté for one more minute continually stirring (be careful not to burn the garlic).

Add the Jerusalem artichokes and parsnips, and sauté for a few minutes over a gentle heat.

Add the stock gradually. You may not need all of it, as Jerusalem artichokes are very watery when cooked. Bring to the boil.

Season with salt and pepper, cover and cook for 30 minutes over a low heat until the artichokes and parsnips are very tender.

Purée the soup in a food processor or using a hand stick blender. Better yet, it is best to put through a blender so that you can gauge the amount of liquid required. If using a hand blender, pour out some liquid first (it's easier to add liquid then to remove it later).

Add the coconut yogurt (if needed), taste and adjust the seasoning.

Remove the skin of the parsnips, discard, then continue peeling the parsnips so you get strips of the length of parsnip.

Pre-heat the sunflower in a medium deep saucepan. You will need to fill the saucepan half-way with oil. In batches, drop in a handful of the thinly sliced parsnips, and as soon as the vegetable crisp starts to change colour, remove from the hot oil using a slotted metal spoon. Place on kitchen paper and sprinkle with some sea salt, and repeat with the remaining batches.

Garnish the soup with the parsnip crisps.

LISA'S TIP

If you'd like to make a Jerusalem artichoke risotto, keep the puréed vegetables from the beginning stages and freeze to use when needed.

Cottage Pie

There's a reason why this dish has remained a classic – it is incredibly satisfying. This version is dairy free.

{serves 4 - 6}

ingredients

4 potatoes (approx. 900g) cut into quarters
500g lean minced beef
2 enchalion shallots, finely chopped
1 tbsp tomato purée
3 tbsp tomato ketchup
2 tsp Worcestershire sauce
2 tbsp sunflower oil
30g coconut oil
sea salt
white and black pepper
garlic granules

Preparation time - 40 mins, cooking time - 30 mins

Preheat the oven to 375°F, gas mark 5, 190°C (170°C fan-assisted).

Put the potatoes in a large saucepan of lightly salted water and bring to the boil.

Reduce the heat slightly and simmer for 15-20 minutes until potatoes are soft.

Drain through a colander, then mash through a potato ricer directly back into the saucepan.

Season the potatoes lightly with sea salt and white pepper. Then mash in the coconut oil over a gentle heat for 1 minute, then set aside.

Heat the oil in a non-stick frying pan, add the shallots and cook gently until translucent for 5 minutes or until soft.

Gradually add the minced beef, over a medium heat, breaking up with a wooden spoon, for 5 minutes until browned.

Add the tomato purée, tomato ketchup, Worcestershire sauce and season with garlic granules, sea salt and black pepper to taste.

Continue to cook over a low heat for 10 minutes.

Spoon the beef mixture into a 2 litre baking dish and carefully spoon the mash over the top, spreading over the surface of the filling.

Using a fork, create a pattern over the top of the potato topping.

Bake in the preheated oven for 30 minutes, until heated through and the potato crust is golden.

LISA'S TIP

If you prefer more vegetables, add diced carrots and peas to the beef mixture. You can also substitute celeriac mash for the potatoes if you are trying to maintain a low-carb diet.

Hearty Beef Stew

A rich, satisfying dish that can be made several days ahead of time.
In fact, the flavours are better after a day or two in the fridge.

{serves 4}

ingredients

1kilo boneless braising beef steak, cut into 5cm pieces

2 tbsp sunflower oil

1 onion, finely chopped

1 red onion, finely chopped

3 garlic cloves, finely chopped

3 carrots, cut in half lengthways in diagonal 2.5cm pieces

2 celery sticks cut into 2.5cm pieces

600g Maris Piper potatoes, cut into quarters (rinse under water to release starch)

1 sweet potato, cut into 2.5cm cubes

1 tbsp tomato ketchup

2 tsp Worcestershire sauce

200ml red wine

2 tbsp corn flour

1 bay leaf

850ml beef stock

sea salt and black pepper

paprika

garlic granules

Preparation time - 30 mins, cooking time - 2.5 to 3 hours

Preheat the oven to 325°F, gas mark 3, 160°C (140°C fan-assisted).

In a mixing bowl combine the corn flour, paprika, garlic granules, sea salt and black pepper.

In a heavy based flameproof casserole dish (26cm in diameter), add 1 tbsp sunflower oil, brown the beef in batches for 3-4 minutes or until caramelised on all sides.

Then transfer to the mixing bowl and coat the beef in the seasoned corn flour, set aside.

Heat the remaining oil over a medium heat, add the onions to the casserole dish and cook until translucent for about 5 minutes.

Add the garlic and cook for 1 minute, being careful not to burn it.

And the red wine, turn up the heat a fraction to cook out the alcohol, then reduce the liquid by 50 per cent.

Add the carrots, celery, potatoes and sweet potatoes, then pour in 275ml of the beef stock.

Return the beef to the casserole.

Add the remaining stock, Worcestershire sauce, ketchup and bay leaf.

Bring to a boil, cover with the lid, place in the oven and cook for 2 ½ hours. You should check every 30 minutes, adding stock or water if needed.

After the casserole has been cooking for 2 ½ hours you may need to cook for a further 30 minutes until the beef is completely tender and the sauce has thickened.

Feel free to remove the lid if you want a thicker stew.

Remove the bay leaf and serve.

LISA'S TIP

For me, this is one of the best dishes of Winter – not only is it nourishing, but it makes the house smell wonderful when it is cooking.

Fish Pie

This healthy take on a traditional recipe is wheat, gluten and dairy-free! The celeriac provides a tasty and low-carb alternative to potatoes and the almond milk replaces milk. Enjoy guilt-free!

{serves 4}

ingredients

2 kg celeriac (approx. 2 large), peeled and cut into equal sizes

1 large leek, sliced (keep ¼ layer of leek to wrap the bouquet garni)

1 onion, quartered

1 large bunch of dill

½ celery stalk

7 tbsp coconut oil

3 large eggs

700ml almond milk

500g cod, fillets with skin

500g haddock, fillets with skin

2 tsp horseradish cream

3 tbsp cornflour

¼ tsp nutmeg, ground

sea salt and white pepper

garlic granules

Preparation time - 60 mins, cooking time - 40 mins

Preheat the oven to 375°F, gas mark 5, 190°C (170°C fan-assisted) Peel celeriac, cut into 5cm cubes, and place in a large saucepan. Cover with cold, salted water. Bring to the boil, cover and simmer for 25-30 minutes until tender. Drain and leave to dry in a colander.

In a large non-stick frying pan, add 1 tbsp coconut oil and sauté the sliced leeks until soft. Season with sea salt, white pepper and garlic granules then transfer to a bowl with a little finely chopped dill. Boil the eggs, peel and cut into quarters. Set aside.

To make the bouquet garni, place the large bunch of dill in the middle of the celery stalk, wrap in a small layer of leek, and tie with string. In the large non-stick frying pan add the almond milk, bouquet garni and the onion. Put the pan on a low heat until simmering then insert the fish fillets and cook 5 minutes. With a slotted spoon, lift the fish onto a plate.

Remove the pan from the heat and let the almond milk infuse for 10 minutes then discard the onion and bouquet garni and strain the milk into a large bowl and set aside. To make the topping of the fish pie, place the celeriac in a food processor and blend until smooth. Add 3 tbsp coconut oil 2 tsp horseradish, sea salt and white pepper. Check at this point for seasoning.

Creamy sauce - in a large saucepan heat 3 tbsp coconut oil with 3 tbsp corn flour, when it starts to thicken, remove from the heat. Gradually whisk the strained almond milk into the saucepan, it will be thick at first, but keep whisking and a smooth sauce will come together. Return the pan to the heat and whisk until the sauce thickens. Season generously with sea salt, white pepper, and nutmeg. Add the sautéed leeks to the sauce. In a large ovenproof dish 23cm x 23cm, 7cm high, flake the fish (discard the skin) into chunky pieces. Place in the base of the dish. Pour over the creamy sauce, and arrange eggs around. Cover with the celeriac puree, smooth out and run the tip of a fork up and down the pie to create a nice topping. Bake the pie in the preheated oven for 40 minutes, or until the top is slightly golden. Leave to stand 10 minutes before serving.

LISA'S TIP

Healthy eating doesn't mean giving up on family favourites. If you are vegetarian or vegan, try substituting cauliflower or broccoli for the fish.

Lamb Curry

A succulent lamb dish made easy
by slow-cooking in the oven.

{serves 4}

ingredients

1 kilo lamb (from the shoulder),
cut into 3cm cubes

250g tomatoes (approx. 2 large)
deseeded and cut into thin slices

1 large onion, finely chopped

4 garlic cloves, crushed

400g canned chick peas

400ml coconut milk

2 tbsp sunflower oil

400ml chicken stock

1 tbsp fresh ginger grated

1 tbsp corn flour

½ tsp cumin seeds

¼ tsp chilli flakes

1 ½ tbsp garam masla

1 tsp ground coriander

2 tsp turmeric

sea salt and black pepper

1 tsp tomato purée

1 tsp coconut sugar

garnish

fresh coriander, one bunch

160ml coconut cream

wholegrain rice

Preheat the oven to 350°F, gas mark 4, 180°C (160°C fan-assisted)

In a food processor blend the chopped onion, garlic, ginger and cumin seeds until smooth.

In a large mixing bowl, add the corn flour, chilli flakes, garam masala, turmeric, ground coriander and season with black pepper and sea salt.

Heat a large oval casserole dish (29cm in diameter) and add 1 tbsp sunflower oil and then the lamb. Cook over a high heat for 3-4 minutes, or until the lamb is golden brown all over, then spoon out the lamb into the seasoned flour mixture, coat the lamb using a spoon until all the pieces are covered with the seasoning.

Reduce the heat and add the remaining oil, add the onion mixture and fry on a gentle heat for about 2-3 minutes, remove the pan from the heat and add the seasoned lamb back to the saucepan.

Cook for a further minute then add the chicken stock slowly to deglaze and release any residue at the bottom of the pan. Bring to a boil, then reduce the heat to a simmer and pour in the coconut milk, sliced deseeded tomatoes, sugar and tomato purée.

Cook, covered, in the preheated oven for about 1 hour until the lamb is tender.

Reduce the oven temperature to 325°F, gas mark 3, 160°C (140°C fan-assisted) add the chick peas and cook for a further 1 hour and 45 minutes. Check to see if you need to add liquid from time to time.

Just before serving you can add a spoonful or two of coconut cream if you like.

Serve with wholegrain rice and garnish with fresh coriander.

LISA'S TIP
The intense flavours develop overnight so it is best to make ahead!

Mild Chicken Curry

A luscious but light version of chicken
curry flavoured with coconut.

....

{serves 4 - 6}

ingredients

1 whole chicken cut into 8
pieces (breast into 4, 2 thighs, 2
drumsticks)

2 medium onions finely chopped

1 tbsp ground ginger

1 tbsp turmeric

1 tbsp cumin

1 tsp Madras curry powder

2 cloves garlic, crushed

2 tbsp peanut oil

50g coconut oil or ghee (clarified
butter)

12 tbsp soy or coconut yoghurt

1 400ml can coconut milk

2 tsp coconut sugar

salt and pepper

garnish

fresh coriander

coconut yogurt (coyo)

wholegrain rice

mango chutney on the side

Preparation time - 40 mins, cooking time - 1.5 to 2 hours (chickens
vary in weight - you may need to adjust cooking time)

Preheat the oven to 350°F, gas mark, 180 °C, (160°C fan-assisted).

Cut legs and thighs from the chicken in one piece then cut legs from
thighs. Cut wings from chicken with a small amount of breast meat,
remove and discard the skin from the chicken. Cut breasts from
chicken, cutting through rib bones along each side of the body, cut
close to the backbone, cut breast into quarters, trim away any excess
fat and retain for sealing the chicken).

Mix the spices together in a bowl, peel and crush the garlic. Place a
frying pan on the stove with a little fat from the chicken and seal the
chicken pieces until lightly coloured on all sides. Place all the seared
chicken pieces on a large roasting tray. Season with salt, pepper and
a sprinkle of the spice mix. Add the oil, crushed garlic clove and
massage into the chicken pieces.

Pour a little coconut oil or ghee over each chicken piece and put in the
oven, uncovered, for 30 minutes. In the meantime, chop the onions
and fry over a low heat until soft. Mix the remaining spices together
with the coconut milk, coconut yoghurt, coconut sugar and onions.
When the chicken has been cooking for 30 minutes, take out of the
oven, pour the onion, coconut cream, coconut yogurt and spice mix
over the chicken. Cover with the lid and put back in the oven for
another 40-60 minutes, until done, turning over once, and basting the
juices over the chicken. When cooked, pour in a little coconut yogurt
and stir. Garnish with a little fresh chopped coriander if you wish.

Serve with wholegrain rice and mango chutney.

LISA'S TIP

*Curry can be made 3 days ahead, kept covered in the refrigerator or
can be frozen up to 2 months. You can replace chicken with other meat,
or turn it into a vegetarian dish. If you have leftovers you can either
chop up the chicken into a coronation chicken salad - just toss in some
lettuce, raisins and flaked almonds with a coconut and mango dressing
with a touch of vinegar and off you go!*

Ossobuco

This is my ultimate signature dish! When my family ask 'what's for dinner?' and the answer is Ossobuco, I know there's going to be a full house! Serve with creamy polenta.

{serves 6}

ingredients

8 pieces of veal shin

1 red onion, sliced into half moons

1 white onion, sliced into half moons

4 garlic gloves crushed

75g corn flour

1 tsp boullion

1 chicken stock cube

570ml of boiling water

2 tsp honey

4 carrots, sliced half lengthways and then slice x2

8 tbsp tomato pasta sauce

4 tbsp sweet red wine

4 tbsp olive oil

sea salt, white pepper and black pepper

garlic granules

paprika

garnish

serve with polenta, cook as directed on packaging

Preparation time - 40 mins, cooking time - 2.5 hours

Preheat the oven to 375°C, gas mark 5, 190°C (170°C fan-assisted).

Wash and pat dry the pieces of veal shin.

Season each piece with garlic granules, paprika, salt and white pepper on both sides on a chopping board.

Lightly cover each piece in corn flour.

In a casserole dish, fry onions with 2 tbsp olive oil until translucent, then remove from the dish.

Over a gentle heat, seal the veal shins in 2 tbsp olive oil for 20 seconds on each side, then remove onto a plate.

Add the red wine to deglaze the corn flour from the bottom of the dish.

Add the sautéed onions, carrots and crushed garlic, tomato sauce, honey and season with salt and pepper.

Add the veal shins to the casserole dish, together with the chicken stock and bouillon.

Place, covered, in the oven and bake for 2.5 hours, checking every 50 minutes, turning over the veal and basting the juices.

Serve on a bed of polenta.

LISA'S TIP

At the end of the cooking time, take the lid off to check the meat for tenderness, by gently prodding it with a spoon and remove from the heat but keep warm. This dish is my all time favourite!!! LOVE LOVE LOVE! (You had me at 'hello' with this dish)

Raw Tiramisu

The Italian standard elevated
to a decadent level.

....

{makes 16 slices}

base

200g blanched whole almonds

100g whole almonds (with skins)

150g macadamia nuts

300g soft medajool dates, remove
stones

1 tbsp coconut oil

sea salt, pinch

topping

300g cashews, unsalted soaked in
water overnight

2 tbsp coconut oil

2 tbsp agave nectar

120ml almond milk

1 tsp vanilla bean paste

2-3 tsp Nescafé espresso freeze
dried coffee powder

3-4 tbsp Amaretto liquor

garnish

30g cocoa powder, sifted over the
cake

50g dark chocolate shavings

Preparation time - 40 mins, soaking (8 hours) plus freezing time 2-3 hours

Soak the cashews overnight for 8 hours with enough water to cover. (this method helps to soften and blend well to get the creamy texture)

Line the base and sides of a square 8 ½ inch by 8 ½ inch loose bottom tin with parchment paper.

In a food processor, blend the almonds and macadamia nuts, until roughly chopped, then pour into a mixing bowl.

Remove the stones from the medajool dates, and place into the food processor, and blend until smooth.

When the dates are smooth add the coconut oil and a pinch of sea salt together with roughly chopped almonds and macadamia nuts, and blend until combined (do not over blend, as you want to keep a little texture to the base).

Press this mixture into the base of your tin, then smooth out with the back of a spoon until completely level.

Then place in the freezer to harden up whilst you make the filling.

Pass the cashews, which have been soaked over night, through a sieve and run under cold water, then drain on kitchen towel to remove excess water.

To make the filling in the food processor, add the soaked cashew nuts and blend for 3 minutes until smooth, wipe down the sides, add the coconut oil and blend for further 2 minutes, keep wiping down the sides so all the cashews are blended.

In a measuring jug, add the almond milk, agave nectar, coconut oil, coffee (I used 2 tsp. coffee, although you can add more), amaretto (I used 3 tbsp. amaretto, although you can add more), and vanilla bean paste.

Beat the mixture with a small hand whisk or fork so that everything is thoroughly blended.

LISA'S TIP

I love tiramisu. Seriously...it's the perfect not too sweet, light and creamy treat - dessert does not have to be a guilt-ridden pleasure. This one is delicious and full of precious nutrients and it's wonderful as it's dairy free, with no added preservative or additives. Do not eat the whole thing in one sitting though. I know, it is going to be very tempting!

Blend the cashew mixture again, slowly pouring in the milk mixture until everything is combined, check for taste - you might need more coffee or amaretto.

Remove the base from the freezer, then carefully spoon the mixture into the tin, make sure again that the filling is smooth and level.

Place back in the freezer for 2-3 hours.

When ready to serve, remove from the freezer, sprinkle with sifted cocoa powder and garnish with chocolate shavings.

Cut into 16 slices when you're ready to serve. You can either keep this dessert in the freezer or in the refrigerator.

Gluten-free Chocolate Banana Cake

A real showstopper with its crushed banana chips and
shaved chocolate. The frosting is dairy-free, too.

{serves 12}

ingredients

1 tsp espresso coffee powder

1 tsp boiling water

4 large eggs, beaten

175g coconut sugar

1 tsp vanilla bean paste

100g fine cornmeal

150g dark chocolate, melted

2 ripe bananas, mashed

chocolate covering

200g dark chocolate melted

50g coconut oil

250ml soya single cream

80g banana chips, crushed

50g dark chocolate shavings

Preparation time - 30 mins, cooking time - 30 mins, decorating time 30 mins

Preheat the oven to 310°F, gas mark 3, 160°C (140°C fan-assisted).

Rub some oil on 2 x 20cm (8inch) round cake tins, and line the base with parchment paper.

Dissolve espresso with the boiling water, set aside. Melt the chocolate in a glass bowl over hot simmering water. Then set aside to cool. Beat the eggs and coconut sugar with a electric beater until light and fluffy. Add the vanilla bean paste and coffee mixture. Gradually add the fine cornmeal to the egg mixture.

When the chocolate has cooled, add the mashed bananas. Fold the chocolate and mashed bananas into the egg mixture until combined. Divide the mixture between the two cake tins and bake on the middle shelf for 30 minutes. Remove from the oven and leave to cool in the tins for 10 minutes, then turn out onto a wire rack to cool, then either cover tightly with foil or continue to decorate.

To make the icing, melt the chocolate as above, then slightly cool and stir in the coconut oil and then the cream. To assemble the chocolate covering, place one half of the cake on your serving platter. Using a palette knife, spread a layer of the chocolate icing on the cake, then sandwich together.

Cover the sides and top of the cake with the icing carefully with a warmed palette knife. Fill in any gaps. The sides/top should be straight and even. Scatter the crushed banana chips around the sides of the cake and decorate the top with chocolate shavings. Allow the cake to sit at room temperature, covered by a cake dome or a large glass bowl, for at least two hours before serving. The flavours will improve and get better with time.

LISA'S TIP

This is a lovely, moist cake, which is sometimes hard to achieve with gluten-free flour! When you pull the cake out of the oven, it will look like it's not done in the centre. Don't worry, that's correct!

Florentines

The combination of dried fruits, cornflakes, all held together by sweetened condensed milk is magic to the taste buds. For extra indulgence why not coat the base or drizzle the top with melted white, milk or dark chocolate.

{makes 40 - 50}

ingredients

250g corn flakes
200g salted peanuts
200g raisins
397g condensed milk

chocolate covering

50g dark chocolate, melted

Preparation time - 40 mins, cooking time - 12 to 13 mins

Pre-heat the oven to 300°F, gas mark 2, 150°C (130°C fan-assisted). Line two large baking trays with parchment paper.

In a large mixing bowl add the cornflakes, raisins & salted peanuts.

Pour over the condensed milk. Using a wooden spoon, carefully ensure that the corn flakes are coated with the condensed milk.

I use 30g of mixture and a teacup to make the Florentines. Using a teaspoon, press mixture into the base. Then flip onto your pre-lined baking tray (occasionally dip the cup into a bowl of cold water, to help the Florentines slide out).

Bake in the preheated oven for 12-13 minutes, watching to ensure that they don't burn.

Remove from the oven, leave to cool on the tray then transfer to a wire rack to cool completely.

Melt the dark chocolate and drizzle over the Florentines.

LISA'S TIP

These are a favourite festive delight, that will quickly be devoured at any time in our household. A great treat for children to get involved in making and they don't cost a lot too! If you find making the Florentines too technical, you can line the sides and base of 25cm square tin with parchment paper and press the mixture into the tin and bake, then you can cut into squares.

Raw Chocolate Mousse Cake

A silky mousse cake with a crunchy base and the
wonderful flavours of chocolate and coconut.

{serves 12 -14}

crust ingredients

100g pistachio nuts

150g blanched almonds

50g desiccated coconut

200g dates, (pre soak if hard)

3 tsp lemon juice

1 pinch sea salt

chocolate covering

200g dark chocolate

2 x 400ml coconut milk, full fat
canned (keep refrigerated)

1 x 160ml coconut cream (keep
refrigerated) reserve 2 tsp for
garnish

3 tbsp date syrup

2 tsp custard powder

garnish

2 tsp coconut cream, whipped
taken from above

Preparation time - 60 mins, freezing time 20 mins

Line the base and sides of 20cm non-stick springform tin with parchment paper.

Place the pistachios, blanched almonds and desiccated coconut into a food processor and pulse until a chunky sandy consistency. Place into a clean bowl. Add the dates, lemon juice and salt to the food processor, blend until smooth.

Add the pistachio nut mixture back into the food processor, and blend until it forms a ball. Place the nut and date mixture into your prepared tin, press down firmly on the base and one inch around the sides and place in the freezer. Remove the coconut milk cans from the fridge, turn them upside down and open the 'wrong end' up (the milk will separate from the cream in the fridge). Pass the coconut milk and cream through a sieve (you only want to use the hard part of the coconut, discard the milk for this recipe). Spoon into a food mixer or use an electric hand held whisk. Beat for about 4-5 minutes, stopping occasionally to wipe down the side of the bowl.

Melt the chocolate over a water bath for one minute then add the date syrup and custard powder. Leave to cool then add the cream. Slowly fold the cream mixture into the chocolate, mix well (keeping 2 tsp of the whipped cream aside). If the chocolate gets hard and gritty when folding in the whipped coconut cream, don't panic, just place the bowl back over the water bath and stir until smooth.

Remove the nut base after 20 minutes from the freezer. When the chocolate mixture is smooth, pour into the nut base. Smooth out the chocolate mixture. Drizzle 2 tsp whipped coconut cream over the top of the chocolate mousse and then, using a fork, carefully mix up the coconut cream into the chocolate to get a marble effect.

Keep refrigerated once made.

LISA'S TIP

If you LOVE chocolate as much as I do, then this is for you. Yes it is possible to prepare the chocolate mousse from only a couple of ingredients without, dairy, cream or eggs! Make sure you refrigerate the cans of coconut milk and cream overnight to solidify and separate.

Recipe Index

Autumn

Winter

Acknowledgements

To my wonderful family

Thanks to all of you who have contributed their time, knowledge and experience and taken on duties of chief tasters…

My gratitude and thanks go to the following people in no particular order for their support, encouragement and inspiration.

Mum, Dad my dedication says it all, although here is another place to say thank you for believing in this exciting adventure. Grandma Jackie, you've been such an instrumental figure in my life, like a second mum to me, thank you for sharing your recipes and enjoying my cakes, even if they have been gluten-free (although I think I have finally converted you!). To my brother Danny Roukin, thank you for all your constructive criticism, and I have noted when you're around 'not too much salt or sugar'! To my sister-in-law Liat Roukin, thank you for always being happy to receive food deliveries in return for your feedback, and I look forward to cooking with my nephews, Eitan & Ori Roukin. To my close cousins who have played a very important role in my life. Thank you Michelle Burns being a 'sister', you've been through my ups and downs, yet you've always been there for me and we've shared fabulous food around the world together. Thank you to another 'sister', Rebekah 'Shaman' Bloom for her continued support, encouragement and inspiration. Thank you to Jo and Mitch Kaye for being my first students and their continued enthusiasm. Thank you, Harriet and David Bloom, for always believing in me. Thank you Lawrence Bloom, Janet Bloom, Lynda Burns and all my extended family for your ongoing loving support.

To my wonderful and friends, so many of you have helped me throughout the good and bad times, although I think it has made our relationships stronger. Thank you for also being my chief tasters, Abi and Gemma Rogers, I can always count on one of the Roger's sisters liking one of my recipes! Thank you Samantha Norman for our long walks and talks about food and relationships. Thank you Emma Eker for your valuable knowledge and support. Thank you Katie Waxman for your love and being a strategy sounding board. Thank you to my dinner party girls, Charlotte Bentley, Vicky Baruch and Samantha Richards, for sharing delicious food and great chats.

Huge thank you to my special friend Kemal Alam, you've been influential from the beginning.

A further thank you to Tammy Poggo, Jo Brook, Sasha Cedar, Denise Peters, Sasha Goldsmith, Tracey Wander, Matt Florin, Marcelo Sanchez, Sacha Isaacs, Marc Lewis, Lex Van Dam, Leonard Charlton, Tanya Selkus, Lisette Lewis, Hiliary Natoff, Xenia Capsalis, Sam Hill, Perry Field and Lisa Halpern.

To my wonderful team who've brought this cookbook to life. Thank you. Tracey Tannenbaum for stepping into my shoes; you've been my personal guardian and you've delivered my story in such a beautiful way. To my team at Spiffing Covers, James Willis, Richard Chalkley and Stefan Proudfoot, thank you all for your creativity and pulling this whole book together, I may have driven you mad at times, but we made it happen. To my food photographer, David Munns, as soon as I saw your incredible talented work, I knew you were the best person for this cookbook; everyone is already salivating over

Acknowledgements

your amazing pictures. Thank you Victoria Allen for the use of your amazing props, I was immensely upset to return everything! A massive thank you to my food stylist, Emily Kydd, my lifesaver, so talented and made all my recipes with love and brought them to life. Thank you Rina Steinberg, my make-up artist for making me look refreshed and glowing, if only you could make me up every day! Thank you to my wardrobe stylist Jude Lobb, for styling me in a comfortable and stylish, elegant way (loving my new wardrobe)! You have all been extremely talented and supportive in your own areas and I most certainly couldn't have wished for a better team. I couldn't have done this book without you all.

To my pillars of support for wisdom, guidance and encouragement when I needed reassurance, a huge thanks to KP for influencing me that life is not a sprint it's a marathon. Thank you, Dr. Eric Ansell and Linda Swimer, you've both independently encouraged me to believe in myself.

To my past employers who taught me all the learning curves of business, my deepest appreciation goes to where my career and love of food started with Sylvia & Harold Sobell, Sara Quah, Elayne Mattey, Tony Page, Melvyn Bentley, Jesus Adorno, Natalia Andreyeva and Daniel Herman.

To all the professional chefs & suppliers who have graciously and generously donated their time or their produce. Thank you to Ocado for providing all the ingredients for the *My Relationship with Food* cookbook - Neill Abrams, Arati Nar and Drew Norton. Thank you to my suppliers for their reliable service and advice Yossi at Menachem, Bifulco Butchers, Dominic at JA Corney and John at Panzers Fruit. Thank you to my chef friends Michael Wilding, Dona & Duarte Silva for sharing enthusiasm for recipes and tips.

To my students and institutes who have supported me, thank you to Barbara Mansi, Helen Harris and Anne Melbourne for giving me the opportunity to teach at HGSI, encouraging students to cook. Teaching cookery is like a story. You have wonderful ingredients, a method and then finishing creating something made with love.

Thank you to my students who've enjoyed being taught and for your emails and testimonials. Glad to hear you are continuing to cook my recipes! You can now have 100 recipes in one place! Danielle Shehayek, Simone Suss, Debbie Fireman, Debroah Roberts, Sharon Pollins, Barry Cohen, Elaine French, Jules Gishen, Michael Angel, Janine Asserson, Hazel Avigdori, Libby Avigdori, Mike Leibling, Dafna Reynolds, Renata Grgek, Laura Hilton, Louise Robey and Daniel Levin And a special thank you to Laurence Field and Rachel Creeger at the LJCC to giving me all the wonderful opportunities of working closing with Fusion children's cookery programs and setting up 'The FUSION Gateways Programme' and huge thank you to Victoria Prever, for your guidance and for featuring my recipes in the JC Newspaper.

To anyone I have left out, I am sorry although I am happy to sign your cookbook with a personalized acknowledgement with my gratitude.

Lisa x